DISASTER MON AMOUR

DISASTER MON AMOUR

DAVID THOMSON

On our love affair with catastrophe,
so long as it is happening to someone else

Yale UNIVERSITY PRESS

New Haven & London

Published with assistance from the foundation established in memory of James Wesley Cooper of the Class of 1865, Yale College.

Yale University Press books may be purchased in quantity for educational, business, or promotional use. For information, please e-mail sales.press@yale.edu (U.S. office) or sales@yaleup.co.uk (U.K. office).

Set in Janson Roman and Felix Titling types by
Integrated Publishing Solutions.
Printed in the United States of America.

Library of Congress Control Number: 2021934648
ISBN 978-0-300-24694-0 (hardcover : alk. paper)

A catalogue record for this book is available from the British Library.

This paper meets the requirements of ANSI/NISO Z39.48-1992
(Permanence of Paper).

10 9 8 7 6 5 4 3 2 1

For Mathew

When he woke in the woods in the dark and the cold of the night he'd reach out to touch the child sleeping beside him.

—CORMAC MCCARTHY, *The Road*

Old lady: When does the story start?
Author: Now, Madame, at once. You'll soon have it.

—ERNEST HEMINGWAY, *Death in the Afternoon*

Man cannot be free if he does not know that he is subject to necessity.

—HANNAH ARENDT, *The Human Condition*

Yesterday is dead, tomorrow hasn't arrived yet.

—GROUCHO MARX

CONTENTS

DISASTER MON AMOUR

Mon amour?
Don't we ache for romance at the
end of days?
As if it offered a chance of escape?

OVERTURE FOR TWO STAIRCASES

At first there is a sparse piano refrain, halting yet lyrical. It seems to know.

It understands the screen-filling spectacle of two naked bodies, writhing and caressing. As if their tenderness and its wish to be touched was the last thing left.

We do not see faces; we are not asked to identify with their romance. But we interpret them as somehow ancient—or far ahead in the future. It's not easy to tell one era from another. Ecstatic bodies, abandoned yet yearning, provide our most enigmatic rapture, waiting for death or striving to be born. It is not just that they are "making" love, or lifelike love. They want to have us faithful to the church of amour. You can decide that the pinnacles of cinema are disaster and rapture, and so they are twinned—"Thus with a kiss, I die," is from *Romeo and Juliet*, when another meaning of "die" was the prospect of sexual coming. So alive; so near the end.

These two seem coated in sand or silica. It is a crystalline dust on their skin, as if they had been buried once or were statues made from molten ore. It was 10,000 degrees in Hiroshima, August 5, 1945.

A man's voice says, "You saw nothing at Hiroshima."

I did, a woman protests, so innocent and loving.

They are speaking French, but he is Japanese. She tells him about the museum she went to, four times, in Hiroshima—the photographs, the twisted metal, the hair that fell out. The piano picks up wistful wind instruments. Then it lurches into a drunken waltz to match the fun of the museum. There were children taking in the show there.

The bodies become natural now: the sand has given way to carnal sweat. A Japanese man and a French woman.

Doesn't Hiroshima count as a disaster?

Hiroshima Mon Amour, 1959, a film by Alain Resnais and Marguerite Duras.

So lovely, so terrible.

◆

May 6, 2020. People are celebrating the anniversary of victory in Europe. Although few were aware of it as yet, on May 6, 1945, Hitler was dead. Seventy-five years ago. It was said that things would return to normal. But of all the people alive in 1945, none lives on like Hitler. The tread of monsters is heavy in our sleep.

In the 2020 room of pomp, with flags and an aircraft-carrier desk, a president is holding an audience with health care workers— this is as close as he will get that day to a hospital or a morgue. One nurse—a head of nursing—is admitting nervously that protective gear can be "sporadic." She has worn the same mask for weeks.

The president looks at her, and then as his slowing wits realize what she is saying, he turns away. Rejecting her. He cannot be seen attending to her or her experience. He denies what she says—he has been told other stories. But we need to notice the bestial gloom in his sunken face, the sullen misery, the childish folding of his arms, the way in which he is not getting his way.

This is hideous. We had elected evil—his only talent.

Oh yes, that was long ago, before he took to the road, when we should have seen he was an act, the bully, a surly dinosaur, such a fraud we were stupid to be afraid. But fear can conquer reason.

◆

What do we mean by disaster? I know, it could be the ultimate smashup, a knockout blow to all our hopes.

Or it could be that as I'm meeting a girl I might be in love with I bend down to pick a flower for her and the seam in my pants rips! She starts to laugh at me (as if I'm Hardy and she is Laurel). This is not unkind. She can't help it. Comedy can be a killer. But as I turn my back, somehow, somewhere, the big one goes off. At first I think it must be a Richter 7.9, but then I realize it's the nuclear fireball. A thousand miles away, but approaching. How had I forgotten that, going out with a girl?

I'm seventy-nine—that's a mishap, maybe, waiting on worse. I'm English by birth, education, language, and every instinct: it is my realism. But now I'm a citizen in San Francisco, as removed from realism as America itself. I've been in a 6.9, and here I am in the moment of Covid-19. Yet I am calling this book *Disaster Mon Amour* because the fearsome possibilities cannot escape some irony or romance that may amount to beauty. It's as if in crisis we can feel history rolling over us like a gorgeous wave. For all our dread, it has become a show with old-fashioned mourning turned to shining black humor.

So I'm thinking about our attitude to disaster, our terror and our attraction. I'll try to keep a straight line with the argument, but I should warn you that a crucial rhythm in disaster is the unexpected. So the form of this book cannot simply be sequential. It responds to how cinema, the movies, can cut, just like that, from a flower to pants splitting to girlish laughter to 10,000 degrees. One surprise after another.

I am reminding you of that. I am hired in because I am supposed to write about film. And so I will. But films go from *a* to *b* in a flash, or from *c* to *w* like magic. We have to keep up. You will be hoping that Covid-19 could inspire the remaking of America's dream, and not just the monster's dumb fantasy of making it great again.

CUT and SUTURE. Every sudden edit is a marriage.

I'm looking at two staircases, and while that household convenience is a cute, useful shape in our lives, still you don't have to be seventy-nine to know that steps can be a perilous place.

It's the spring of 1932 in Los Angeles, a sunny day. Stan Laurel and Oliver Hardy have reassessed their financial situation and invested their $3.80 in a cart and a horse. They are in the hauling business now, so when a bourgeois lady buys a player piano, they are the guys who will deliver it to her home, 1127 Walnut Avenue.

I am looking at a 29-minute film, *The Music Box*, produced by Hal Roach and directed by James Parrott. We honor those names, but truly it's a Laurel & Hardy picture. It proved a great success—it won an Oscar—because it's a disaster waiting to happen, poised like a hummingbird or a kiss.

The boys are taken aback to find a long exterior set of steps leading to 1127. A passing mailman tells them it's the house at the top of the steps. So they are going to get the boxed piano off their cart and then carry it up the stairs. The trigger in this movie is our guessing this will lead to calamity.

CUT to Odessa in Ukraine. In 1837–41, a splendid set of two hundred wide steps was constructed there as a threshold to the city. In *Battleship Potemkin* (1925), Sergei Eisenstein would use those steps as the stage for a massacre in which tsarist troops suppressed an innocent public demonstration. The citizens wanted to support a mutiny on the *Potemkin*, where the living conditions for the crew were appalling. Such an event did not exactly happen (though there was a skirmish on the steps in the 1905 uprising), but that hardly matters now because the Steps sequence has become proverbial.

CUT to Walnut Avenue. The boys are in trouble: it's such a long haul on a warm day. They do their best to carry the box up the steps, but the problems build and at every attempt they drop the box and have to watch it slide all the way down again. Its keys tremble like a carillon of distant bells.

A nanny comes down with a baby carriage (please make a note of this) and so they must go down again politely to let her pass. Our glee is mounting (it's nothing less) not just at the chumps' inept efforts (and we love them both) but because we cannot help anticipating the further reduction of the box and its piano to matchwood. Put it this way: if we were there on the steps we wouldn't think to help or intervene because that would mean stopping the disaster we anticipate and adore. Once you start to come, you must not stop. The longer we stare at Janet Leigh, going from Phoenix to Fairvale, the more we know her drive is fatal.

CUT to Odessa. The crowd on the steps is variegated and amiable, waving to the ship in the harbor. We see a crippled urchin but it's a middle-class crowd, with the expressive faces Eisenstein appreciated—faces like actors. When the soldiers appear at the top of the steps, their uniformity is emphatic: they wear black boots and riding breeches, white tunics and military caps. They carry rifles with fixed bayonets, and when they move forward—as a single unit—it is evident that they intend to clear the steps. The crowd do not immediately sense their danger, so we would like to warn them. But we realize there is no use in that—they are *there* but not in our *here*—so we can settle down as onlookers.

CUT to Los Angeles, where we have a similarly privileged position; we are the spectators ready for fun. Now a man comes down the steps, full of fussy, plump self-importance. He wears a frock coat and a top hat and carries a handsome cane. He tells them he is Professor Theodore von Schwarzenhoffen (Billy Gilbert) with honorifics after his name. He is vain and pompous and, rather than step aside, he expects the boys to go down the steps again so that he can proceed. There is a minor scuffle and then a lovely shot from above of his liberated top hat drifting and tumbling to the street below. It makes our hearts feel good to see this jerk reduced for our amusement. Stan and Ollie deserve that much glory.

CUT to Odessa—the cutting is acquiring a beat or a pulse like the one Eisenstein managed with film, or what would be called montage. The line of soldiers fires on the crowd. The picture is silent, but the puffs of bright white smoke (applied like props, I think) are jolly. They remind us that guns can be fired as a "salute." We do not *want* the public shot and killed. We have no doubt about the cruelty. But we are hoping to watch the process and we may wonder if a little of the callousness isn't creeping into us too. "Montage" means building, and going upwards; but the subject of the scene is more the opposite of those things— it's about descent, and taking life to pieces. But it doesn't stop because of our horror, and so that mood begins to seem playful. The bursts of smoke are rumors of orgasm—we have always been eager for film violence.

At last, in Los Angeles (I apologize, I forgot to call CUT), after three times when the box bounces down to street level, the pair of them get the piano to the top, to the patio of the house. Ollie even steps into the ornamental pool—that's a hoot.

At this point, the gentlest and most philosophical joke arises. That mailman comes by and he marvels at how they labored up the steps with their impossible load when there is a road that circles and bypasses the steep slope. They could have ridden their cart up that road. That's not even the full joke. For now they take their piano downhill again—all the stupid way—so they can ride up to the top. It's not just that disaster befalls these guys; they are intrinsically catastrophic.

That's how we love and understand them. Like those lovers in the silica night.

CUT to Odessa, where real cutting down is coming into play. We are seeing people shot and killed. A young boy in a white shirt is shot. His mother picks him up and moves towards the line of soldiers imploring mercy. So she is herself shot down. There is a baby carriage with a baby inside. Its mother is shot and the unattended carriage begins to bump down the steps. The Cossacks arrive, fierce soldiers on horseback, and they move among the crowd with drawn sabers. We see big close-ups of agonized faces; we see silent screams, the mouths of horror; and spurts of blood where the sabers have struck. We do not see the whole action as a natural spectacle because of the stress on composed shots that are cut together with brilliant timing. There is a deep-seated tension between chaos and control. We feel it, I think, without understanding it. So while the action is cruel, the delivery system of the film enforces that authority without examining its own process.

CUT to Walnut Avenue, where there is no one at home to accept the piano. So the boys seek, somehow, to get the piano inside the house. They are not safe out or in; they might be better off just waiting for Godot. I ask you to believe that this entails a rope-and-pulley system to get the box through an upstairs window. A new kind of mayhem follows, in which bit by bit they start to destroy the house. There is the further consternation of the boys ending up with the wrong hats, so Ollie's bowler is like a dot on his head while Stan's is ready to eclipse his eyes. The box is inside, but when they open it, water from the ornamental pool rushes out to flood the house.

We may ourselves be more or less proud but nervous owners of a "nice" house or apartment, but here we are rocking in mirth (a nice 1932 word) at destruction scenes that would make us frantic if they involved our own home. A curious misalignment is in evidence, an extension of that odd Odessa principle: we love disaster if it happens to others. I realize that may seem obvious or tactless, but I think it is profound if it serves as a protection against catastrophes we are watching.

CUT to Odessa, with corpses on the steps. It is a set piece, but Eisenstein cannot end the sequence like that. So he brings on a finisher that never happened: on realizing what's occurring ashore, the crew of the *Potemkin* train their guns on the city "in retaliation." And so we witness and partake in what will be a common reaction in movies: one disaster is avenged by another (in the name of justice).

The Steps sequence was analyzed and taught for decades as a guide to montage or rapidly edited cinema. This was Soviet, of course, and theoretical, but you can see its dynamism reiterated in just about every American action film. It's part of the principle that damage can be awesome. And gratifying. We can take it for granted that on any witness stand Sergei Eisenstein would have deplored the behavior of the soldiers in Odessa. He was a decent man. But as an artist—and he edited that sequence personally—he was carried away by violence. He is one of the greats.

MEANWHILE in Los Angeles (the steps were real, just south of Silverlake—they are still there), the boys have done their job. There is a brief but lovely dance sequence where they tidy up in time to jaunty music, and Ollie proves a very dainty mover. Then Professor Schwarzenhoffen reappears. He is the man of the house. His wife it was who purchased the piano as a birthday gift for him. But he loathes pianos and is agonized over all the damage; still, he tells his wife that no, he is grateful and fond. He *might* acquire a taste for piano music. You may accidentally burn my stamp collection, my love, accumulated over years at absurd cost—but I will tell you, no matter, I was ready to move on to another hobby (like murder or watercolors).

I hope my crosscutting is intelligible and halfway dynamic—

so it holds you. But it may feel unduly "neat" or contrived. Let me add another optical device, a DISSOLVE, in which different images seem to be swimming in the same sea.

The dissolve was popular once in cinema, and I find it eloquent as a way of relating disparate things—for instance, on a day in June 2020, I found in the newspaper that Covid-19 had set off outbreaks of other maladies because the inoculation services were shut down after the virus. That worry goes beside this wonder, found on Apple News, that two-legged crocodiles maybe ten feet long prowled about 110 million years ago (this is a mere yesterday for some authorities). In South Korea, they have found preserved footprints in the rock of this bipedal croc—he looks an ugly customer in the artist's post-Spielberg interpretation.

Now, you may say this linkage is not just a dissolve; it's a leap. But let me give you one that is far tidier. In 1932, as *The Music Box* opened, Eisenstein was in Los Angeles. It's possible that he met Laurel and Hardy, for he was fond of antic clowns and the boys were authentic stars. Their accounts of calamity made a fortune for them and for the Hal Roach Studio in a year when the Depression (the big-D one) had set in with a vengeance and in ways that would affect the presidential election later in the year.

Eisenstein had come out of the Soviet Union for several reasons: *Potemkin* had been hailed universally; producers in Hollywood sensed the energy in the film, and wondered if they could harness it; and Sergei was growing uneasy with Stalin and the organized ruthlessness of the Soviet economy; he was also finding the stress on moral order in the new regime a restriction on his gay urges. By his early thirties, he could look fifteen years older.

So he came to America and entertained several unlikely possibilities (like every other pilgrim in the movie city). He thought of a film about the discovery of gold at John Sutter's mill in 1848; then he got enthusiastic over a movie drawn from Theodore Dreiser's *An American Tragedy*; and he even went to Mexico, funded in part by Upton Sinclair, to make a movie about Death. That puts it crudely, perhaps, but that's what it amounted to: a ravishingly graphic celebration of the culture of death in an impoverished society. At about the same time, Hemingway laid down his *Death in the Afternoon*. This appeared to be a book about bullfighting, but it was an oratorio on approaching death with accuracy and calm, or the thing Ernest liked to call grace. (I can't do this book without him or that spectral old lady he invented to survey the corrida.)

None of Sergei's ventures came to fruition. So he might have marveled at the wistful dissolve of Laurel and Hardy as sublime and profitable purveyors of physical disaster to a time when so many Americans were witnessing the demolition of their worth and their hope. You can dissolve (if you can't quite cut) from the scene at 1127 Walnut Avenue to the 1932 election, with an assassination attempt on FDR in the weeks between election and inauguration. On February 15, 1933, Joe Zangara fired five shots at the president elect and did kill the mayor of Chicago—because Joe and others were sure Roosevelt was going to be a disaster (or because they meant to kill the mayor?). Weeks later, on March

10, there was a 6.4 earthquake in Long Beach, the first such disturbance in modern Los Angeles (there was a 7.8 in 1680, but the guy there slept through it). The 6.4 was perceived by some as a rebuke to the new president's declaration of a four-day bank holiday.

It is a remarkable function of film and its media to open us up to all the things that are happening at the same time—and to stay wary of drawing conclusions. A CUT seems loaded with meaning, but a DISSOLVE introduces the possibility of doubt or magic.

This isn't just a spiffy double bill, though at 106 minutes it could make a stimulating evening. It's a measure of our constant crosscutting: the way Rachel Maddow in alarm can cut to a babe with an amber waterfall of shampoo hair, or the valor of a Dodge truck on a wild winter hill becoming the Capitol alive with panic. These spasms are always there, like an itch.

IN *SAN ANDREAS*

There is an innocence. There always is. Without it, there is no fall. It feels like life, that hope, the best of times. I daresay 2015 reckoned it was having a tough time, but it had become exquisite five years later.

And on that spur of life, setting out on a fresh venture, an open page, you and I should recognize that we could both be gone before this book is done. That fear of falling need not be fearful, or timid about going on the street, but there is always the chance of a misstep, or an interruption in our sweet motion. Reading a fond text on your phone, you could walk into a pantechnicon. When that vehicle was carrying the overflow of corpses to a secret burial ground or the endless flame of cremation. You heard about such things in New York in the spring of 2020.

So *in the spring and summer of 2019*, I had told a few friends that I was thinking about a book on Disaster. I was speculating on it as a trip or a journey, vague but encouraging, when walking all alone in the countryside seemed so appealing.

Ah, that's interesting, my friends said, their eyes and minds wide open, like kids going on holiday. They saw the point quickly: how we contemplate disaster more and more, as if entranced, while having mixed feelings about it. That could be a lot of fun— it was a genre by now, an edifice of special effects, with the likelihood that the structure and its CGI virtuality was going to come down, like the Golden Gate bridge hit by a tsunami in the movie *San Andreas* (2015), and in another half a dozen films in recent years. That lovely bridge of ours (opened in 1937) does movie push-ups now to be playful, and San Franciscans regard these tricks with glee, not to mention a certain pride. But it's still the solid span I take driving over to the Marin headlands, and the grail of Point Reyes. I'd hate to have it collapse.

But that was jauntiness then: *by April 2020* those northern destinations were more closed, and the bridge was often deserted, as if it had been commandeered as a set for a disaster picture. The awe and glee had turned to isolation and fear of waking with a fever. We always guessed such disasters were at hand—in California there is a catalogue of possibilities, the filing system of ominous scenarios.

These scripts can overlap. When the call arose for face masks to combat Covid-19, I had a mask already. It was the one I had bought *in 2018* when smoke from the Camp fire (near a town called Paradise—there was a Pair o' Dice saloon there once) came down on the city, a distance of 145 miles, so the air was acrid and a dirty, faded yellow. I improvised in the cheery way of Californians.

And we are generally optimistic, not just in California, but across the land. We feel it is an American duty, even if sometimes that leaves us absentminded, or mindless. Never mind, if you're going to rebuild San Francisco, like Dwayne Johnson (the Rock) in *San Andreas*, you need a degree of irrationality. Isn't that what worked after 1906?

Thus, *at Easter 2020*, people everywhere, from the governor of Kentucky to the queen of England to my mother-in-law, eighty-seven, living alone on the edge of the desert in Thermal, California, everyone said, "We're going to get through this."

That's understandable, if slightly tiring. It does sound like hard work, without pay or a pension. The temptation grows that maybe we won't—do we, honestly, deserve to get through it? Have we done such a grand job that we've earned another million years (with the chance to cure cancer, write more Mozart operas, and have sex with robots)? Or did those celebrated dinosaurs say to themselves as the asteroid loomed (this scene needs to be done in slow motion, I think), "Time for some peace, being out of the limelight, and not having to be so damn fearsome night and day." No, the dinos weren't into chat (or not until the era of animated movies), but they're in a cartoon strip now, and so we may be, too, the CGI stick figures on a planet called . . . Corona-66.

!

That mark to indicate a break, or a shift in direction, is also a small playful variant on the customary asterisk. You see, I have the urge to do a book that might be remarked on as "unexpected," "funny," or even delightful. Delightful Disaster. Would I or Yale dare that as a concept?

There will be questions of taste. There often are. The human race may be charging along, brave and indefatigable, or simply lucky, but no one can claim the effect is always respectable.

This delicate balance comes with a film like *San Andreas*, which, when I saw it in San Francisco, played to merry whoops and cheers. As if my fellow citizens were supposed to be so heartless about stick figures, hectic digital flickers, perishing in new inventive ways. But if I have credentials as a film writer, and if there is still a culture of film commentary, then I need to say something about disaster movies. And if only to make you smile, I will say that *Heaven's Gate*, a film I like a lot, was immediately classified as a disaster in film history. Not because several characters are cruelly slaughtered, including a young Isabelle Huppert. Not because it traces the bitter struggle for control of the wooded prairies. But because, in 1980, the film directed by Michael Cimino cost $44 million and earned back $3.5 million. That gap was so wide that the studio, United Artists, tumbled into it and ended its useful life in film history. That was a bad thing, though nearly everyone survived.

By contrast, *San Andreas*, is nowhere near as "good" a film, but it is a far more emphatic entertainment. It cost $110 million and earned $474 million. And I think from the moment the picture opened, its delightfulness had to do with the insolent contrast between its depicted catastrophe and the clear prospect that the film was going to get away with it, and hurry to any bank left standing.

There is a San Andreas fault, a considerable crack in the ground, and it's a presence for California akin to the Pacific yet more menacing. It is a reason for being wary of living in the state, for the fraught meeting place of two tectonic plates cannot give up on their violent affair. In 1989, my wife Lucy and I had a 12-day-old son on the day of the Loma Prieta earthquake. Just after five o'clock in the afternoon, I was preparing to watch game 3 in the World Series between our San Francisco Giants and our Oakland Athletics. It had been a perfect day, hot, sun-drenched and very still, which is not common in the Bay Area. I was ready to watch the game on television. And I was heard to call out to Lucy, in another room—she was changing Nicholas on a table—that all over the country people would be watching and agreeing that the Bay Area was a grand place to be.

It hit at 5:04 p.m., and it was a 6.9 centered a few miles north of Santa Cruz, to the south of the city. The windows at the end of our apartment went from rectangular to diamond shape and then back to rectangular. I believe that is not possible, but that information does not compete with the certainty of what I saw. We wrapped Nicholas in blankets and took him down to the street, where neighbors were gathering. We all agreed that it was reckless to live in the Bay Area with a new baby. We were sure about it. But then we stayed; we loved the city, and believed gambling instincts were expected in California.

The Loma Prieta quake was modest, whatever we felt about it at the time. It caused some damage on the Bay Bridge; an East Bay freeway was flattened in one section; there were ruined buildings in the Marina area of the city. Sixty-three people were killed, which is a good deal fewer than a city manager might have settled for at the height of the tremors. But this was action on the San Andreas fault, and it followed many small tremors in the decade preceding 1989. Later we told ourselves that we had felt something was coming, and the rare hot stillness of the day (October 17) was called "earthquake weather." A legend spread that dogs had started barking before the quake; another claimed they had fallen into hushed awe.

It was the same fault that had caused the 1906 earthquake—the notorious "big one." That had come at 5:12 in the morning and it is reckoned to have been a 7.8. The damage was far greater than in 1989, because fires broke out that were too much for a fire department with horse-drawn "engines." At least 3,000 people died in 1906, and three-quarters of the city was destroyed.

There is a movie that includes that big one—*San Francisco* (1936). It's a story about high life on the turn-of-the-century Barbary Coast, with Clark Gable as a saloon owner and Spencer Tracy as a priest, and both are fond of a singer, embodied as the implausible but endlessly vivacious Jeanette MacDonald. It's black-and-white (it had to be), and it's an MGM romance of its era, trying to defy 1930s Depression and keep us happy. You have to realize that in 1936 "disaster" was offscreen. It was seldom a topic for movies. Disaster then was confined to King Kong running amok, or Laurel & Hardy in the hauling business.

Still, there comes a moment near the end of the film, after MacDonald has sung "San Francisco," that the earthquake strikes. The actuality of five o'clock in the morning is dispensed with in what I'm sure the makers of the film called "the Quake sequence." It is about five minutes and it is a rapid montage of elected and manageable details. Pillars falling from buildings; anguished faces staring up at the mayhem; small constructions seeming to wobble as their platform or the camera were agitated; a lot of crash-bang-screams of fear, and citizens being discreetly crushed. The energy of the sequence is in the editing, not the subject matter. This creative scheme was led by Tom Held and John Hoffman, though the zest and the rhythm is probably due to the uncredited assistant, Slavko Vorkapich, who was a genius at dynamic montage. There is one shot of a new crack widening in a street, but it's plainly a trick shot done on a sound stage. There is one elaborate tall building that comes to pieces in a well-behaved way, a set built specially. But there is no panoramic view of streets and cityscape as razed in the morning light of 1906.

The sequence worked in 1936, and there had been little like it before in fictional filmmaking. But the impact—the tragedy, the shock, the reversal of nature—was not there as it is in so many still photographs taken in 1906 in a feeling that the event and its disorder should be memorialized. And used to cap a blithe, foolish movie scenario. You should recollect that this was at the dawn of another kind of moving picture record, the attempt to convey places like Guernica in Spain, London in the Blitz, Dresden, and then Hiroshima. By that time, innocence had had to shape up fast.

The world was honestly impressed and frightened by the damage revealed in 1945 in newsreels and in movies that happened to be shot in war zones that were recovering so slowly. So you see the shattered Berlin in Roberto Rossellini's *Germany Year Zero* (1948) and you can balance the physical ruin with the demented mind of the small boy at the center of the story. At the same time, for *A Foreign Affair* (a sardonic romance), Billy Wilder had aerial shots of the tumbled down Berlin played against Richard Rodgers's melody "Isn't It Romantic?" In that cute clash—too glib to carry real pain—there was the dilemma of the movies wondering how realistic they could be with catastrophe. Was the show decent?

It was not just that the audience might be upset; there was a considerable sentimental problem in how one might film such horrors. So a ground-zero love story set in Hiroshima in August 1945 would have been a stretch as a must-see, but it put impossible demands on the camera in showing us that ground zero. *Dr. Strangelove* (1964, two years after the very edgy Cuban missile crisis) was a scathing comedy about attitudes towards nuclear disaster, but its most frightening scenes occurred in the war room with human fools in charge.

The Poseidon Adventure (1972) was a famous hit disaster flick, enabled by the way an upside-down ship could be managed as a self-contained and safe set on a sound stage at Twentieth Century–Fox. *Earthquake* (1974) was startling in its day as it required Charlton Heston to rescue Geneviève Bujold from the seething wreckage of Los Angeles. On a budget of $7 million and the boost of a 9.9 on the Richter scale, it employed many clever models, shots of shaking structures, and details of collapsed masonry and horribly endangered civilians. It also used Sensurround in some theatres to simulate the sound and pressure of rumbling. The picture made more than ten times what it had cost. It won an Oscar for sound and a special award for visual effects. This despite a storyline that was as perfunctory as it was clichéd—but maybe everyone behaves like an idiot in a disaster? The threat of earthquake hung over Los Angeles (it always does—there had been a 6.6 in the San Fernando Valley in 1971). But a more common disaster in that city was marital breakdown, and in the film Heston dies with the wife he no longer loves (Ava Gardner), while his true love, Bujold, looks on.

Earthquake was part of a craze in those early '70s—it included the *Planet of the Apes* series, *The Poseidon Adventure*, *Airport*, and *The Towering Inferno*—in which allegedly lifelike renderings of physical destruction seemed a relief from the steady television reportage of Vietnam, where damage was commonplace, not special. But those hyped classics look comic now, not just because of the feeble human stories but because the special effects seem from the Dark Ages. The real story at work was the cultural transition for movies from reality to a simulacrum of things no one had ever seen. The medium went from being photographic to virtual, and disaster took flight on innovative wings. It was akin to performance shifting from theatre to movies.

Over a period of about twenty-five years, bridging the millennium, the cinema moved from the state of mind that grappled with showing actuality—as evident in Steven Spielberg's earnest combat in *Saving Private Ryan*—to existing in a fantasy stretch where reality had yielded to whatever a computer could generate. It is as if we've elected to give up on being surprised by light, life, and nature in favor of digital possibilities. This was not quickly identified, but in the shift the movies had gone from a tenuous, flirty grasp on reality (and humanism) to the reckless lyricism of invention (like an infant president wondering aloud whether disinfectant might blast Covid-19 from our lungs). Disaster became less an interruption than a new giddy norm. The long-term implications of that (and the hint that "term" has been canceled) are fundamental to this book.

Let's concentrate on *San Andreas* first. It's easy to laugh at the film's storyline, its energetic melodrama, and its push-button characters. But make the effort, for the marriage of trite and tidy is essential in its reckoning of disaster.

Ray Gaines is superhuman yet run-of-the-mill—this has always been a favored model in American movies. He is a helicopter rescue pilot in the Los Angeles Fire Department. He is also Dwayne Johnson.

Born in Hayward, California, in 1972, Dwayne played football at the University of Miami as a defensive tackle, but he did not sustain a career in pro football. So he gave up competition for rigged performance. He became a wrestler with the World Wrestling Federation. At six-feet-five and 260 pounds, with a shaved head, a searchlight smile, and a cheerful, self-assertive style, he became a generic figure, the monumental guy, known as The Rock. As such he was a part of the explosive success of wrestling after 2000, and he was a flamboyant exponent of its fake prowess.

Next he went into movies. This is not to criticize him but a way of putting him in a line of heroic performance that extends from Doug Fairbanks by way of Johnny Weissmuller to Sylvester Stallone and Arnold Schwarzenegger. The last in this list shows how easily the hulk might become a governor or more. Thank God for small mercies that Donald Trump has always been physically bogus, from his heeled bone spurs to the crest of his golden lid. Still, he has cultivated the idea of himself as a physical intimidator. He believes in it.

The Rock's Ray is our reliable guy, and his helicopter is wings for his unchallenged fantasy of himself. Not that Ray is going to have an easy day. As the film begins he discovers that his wife Emma (Carla Gugino) is divorcing him. This is hard on their daughter, Blake (Alexandra Daddario), who loves Dad, and is in a lifelong twist because her sister drowned as a child. Of course, Dad blames himself for that. The Rock is immaculate but he's soft at the center.

But the shamelessly adroit script (by Carlton Cuse, after a story by Andre Fabrizio and Jeremy Passmore) has another storyline, crammed with necessary information. Dr. Lawrence Hayes (Paul Giamatti) is a seismologist at Caltech. He is our scientist, rather as Dr. Anthony Fauci became a wizened beacon in the spring of 2020. Hayes is into trying to predict earthquakes—when anyone watching this film has no doubt that they are coming. Prompted by several minor tremors, he goes to Hoover Dam to take some readings, in time for a 7.1.

You may have been to Hoover Dam—it is a wonder, not just a beautiful construction and a grand idea, but a hallowed place, a taut bow of concrete joining rocky outcrops. I have been very moved there, without feeling a hint of a tremor. But we sense the coming gotcha when we hear Hayes lecturing at Caltech about the history of quakes: the 9.1 at Anchorage, Alaska, in 1964, and the 9.5 at Valdivia in Chile in 1960. That one was so powerful that it set off a 35-foot tsunami that washed away the town of Hilo, in Hawaii, nearly seven thousand miles away.

A student asks Hayes what the San Andreas fault (reaching the length of California) means for her, for life, and for civilization. Is it going to go off? Giamatti savors his response, like a huckster selling a sensation: "It's not a matter of *if*, it's a matter of *when!*" Bring it on, the film sighs, fit to be ravished. There is an erotic charge in delivered disaster—it's the deliciousness.

The devastation at Hoover Dam is a sweet marvel. And that is a secret to disaster films—we want our fears of physical ruin rendered as something so beautiful we feel no pain. We know this glee is close to madness, but that is how we play with the prospect of our demise.

So there is a fanatical pursuit of accuracy and realism that imprisons us in fantasy and dissociation. I'm sure the movie took engineering advice on how the dam would buckle and disintegrate. I trust that the laws and properties of concrete have been observed. And the spectacle is profuse and colossal. *San Andreas* is a foolish film, except when it's doing effects, and then it's ecstatic. So it does effects as often as it can. The dam (begun in 1931 and opened in 1936) is made to fracture and subside in a few minutes because of computer-generated imagery, the practice by which set photographs of reality can be shopped and played with in increasingly infinitesimal and infinite ways. There are many films that use CGI in the manner of *San Andreas*, but few that are so unbridled yet so everyday. After all, we have a pretty good idea of what the dam, Los Angeles, and San Francisco were like— before the Fall.

Sitting in the dark, we trust that these structures are still there and safe. We are playing with vicariousness; that is, technologically energized yet not new. For decades we watched immense movie violence and the enactment of lust or desire with the same assurance that such actions were not happening. When Janet Leigh stepped into the shower in *Psycho*, we trembled in anticipation. We wanted to warn her as the apparition of Mother, Mrs. Bates, appeared through the plastic shower curtain. BUT WE DID NOT GO TO HER AID or try to ward off Norman's plunging knife. The real trick play is the conferred irresponsibility and the underlying insight that the most shattering tragedy was contrived or fake. An immense contradiction was being proposed between reality and impossibility. So audiences in Los Angeles and San Francisco, well aware of sitting at ground zero, reveled in the outrage of *San Andreas.*

From Hoover Dam, the movie heads west and then north. We see Caltech models of the state and a line of poppy-red blooms as earthquakes mark out the route. Having rescued his soon-to-be ex-wife (don't ask, just see the movie), Ray abandons a broken chopper, seizes a car, and comes to tranquil midstate fields only to find a gaping ravine in the ground where the fault has picked a fight with the surface. This is a super version of a modest split, a trench, on the Carrizo Plain that has become something of a tourist attraction (rather like the suggested crater in what is now the Yucatan where . . . we'll come to that big one).

What befell LA in *San Andreas* was phenomenal, but the arc of the film is saving San Francisco for its climax. Ray and Emma drive north after his copter has failed. Along the way, by cell phone, they hear from their daughter that Daniel, Emma's husband-elect, abandoned Blake in a cowardly way when she was trapped in an impacted underground parking garage. So Dad and Mom have to rescue her.

They borrow an unused aircraft, and when that falters over a deranged San Francisco, they parachute down to AT&T Park—that's what it was called in 2015. It's Oracle now (for a while at least), but don't bet on these emphatic labels staying in place. Emma has never parachuted before. She clings in Ray's arms as if she is warming up to him again. And when they come to earth at the middle of the infield, Ray is movielike enough to say, "It's been a while since I got to second base with you." One cute guy, with a body of tanned rock. What else could Emma want from a man? Never mind, what the filmmakers want is a spectacle of devastation with cozy human interest.

You can't compare the slick slotting together of the family melodrama with the prodigious yet lyrical passion for the demolition of cities where many of the filmmakers must live. The effects on *San Andreas* were done by several postproduction houses—Hydraulx, Cinesite, and Image Engine. Much of this work was led by Greg and Colin Strause, who have also served as directors (on *Alien vs. Predator: Requiem* and *Skyline*, and many television commercials, including spots for Gatorade and the United States Marine Corps).

But the credits list more than a thousand artisans who had some hand and thought in the film's effects. It's easy to imagine the days and months of concentration and ingenuity that went into their work, and the thrill when they discovered a refinement in the technology that might permit a fresh direction in the story. "Look, we can make the spans of the Golden Gate Bridge turn to strands of limp spaghetti!" These crafts people are as unknown as the stone masons, the woodworkers, and the laborers who put together Gothic cathedrals, but I think they deserve the respect given to more obvious auteurs, like Brad Peyton, who directed *San Andreas*, its several writers, and the many producers who enabled the show.

I find I can watch the disintegration as often as I watch Fred Astaire dance routines, and with a similar exhilaration. It never stales, the drunken tilt and collapse of skyscrapers, the fall that takes away fatigue, the way windows drop like tears, and the crumbling of huge vanities of masonry as if they were dried cake. This is rapture, even if you step back for a moment and realize that it could be so bad for the inhabitants of San Francisco.

And I live there, too, and feel a weird pride over the film. I suspect not many inhabitants of the city past the age of seven failed to see it. (It got a PG-13 rating.) It was Mick LaSalle in the *San Francisco Chronicle* who wrote, "Some movies are easy to mock, but hard to resist. This is one of them."

That's correct, but I think it misses underlying points about our relationship with disaster. The familial reconstruction of the story ignores the urban devastation. It's not just that Ray and Emma will be reunited and reconciled to the loss of one daughter. Meanwhile, Blake chances upon an adorable English boyfriend who has to be the love of her life in the sentimental Richterism of the picture.

So San Francisco is a ghastly mess at the end of the film. But the family unit is solid and survivors are camped on firm wild ground. What do we do? the film asks, and Ray has his line—he has had it from the start, because it's programmed in the ethos and the geology of his rock:

"Now we rebuild."

Old lady: Oh, great heavens, sir, what a wow you have provided! [I should have told you that this old lady had been observing my fitful progress for some time.]

Author: A wow?

Old lady: Indeed! I learned that term watching bullfights in the '20s with Mr. Hemingway. I was there for *Death in the Afternoon*, you may recall. An excitement, a thrill! I did not guess that this *San Andreas* could give me the same lift.

Author: I am happy to have been of service.

Old lady: Forgive me, I had to speak up. But please, get on with your book.

Author: I will, but I believe you are part of it now.

Now we rebuild. That's what rocks tell you, and we may pay lip service to the good intentions in that closure and its togetherness and persistence. That was just five years ago, before Mayor London Breed and Governor Gavin Newsom, and before San Francisco had become—beyond dispute—a city for the high-tech rich (including those who created and executed CGI), a jam of traffic, a spiral of property prices beyond the reach of ordinary citizens, and a mockery to the growing number of homeless on its streets, whose persistence lay in being moved on by the cops and then putting up their tents on another corner as yet unforbidden.

That was before Covid-19 and the early decision (*March 16*) by Sara Cody, medical officer for Santa Clara County, to order sheltering in place in her jurisdiction. This was joined by six other neighboring counties and then rapidly picked up by Mayor Breed and Governor Newsom to shut down the city and the state and flatten the curve of infection. And to save lives. That seemed to work. A month later, it was evident that California had had fewer losses than New York, and other states. But in the full context of 2020, "Now we rebuild" became as bleak and distant as a message in an old bottle, swept up on some shore years after its crisis had been forgotten.

Today as I write—*it is Earth Day, April 22*, the fiftieth anniversary of that gesture—this city like all others is hunched and apprehensive and very broke. The kind of booty that helped generate the revenue on *San Andreas* has nowhere to turn. The largest redistribution of capital in American history is under way—so it is said. So already, *San Andreas* could look as inadvertently forlorn as *San Francisco* once seemed quaint. We have acquired such a misguided mastery of disaster that the process has extinguished so much of meaning itself.

At which point, like a pretty red helicopter hovering between a fatal crash and family reunion, I will tell you that one of the producers on *San Andreas* was Steven Mnuchin, who had been Donald Trump's secretary of the treasury since February 2017 and was in charge of sending out our stimulus checks.

As secretary of the treasury, Mr. Mnuchin earned only $199,700, a sum so modest we have to hope that his profits from *San Andreas* (and from other movie ventures where his Dune company was in partnership with Brett Ratner's RatPac Entertainment) provided a nest egg. I looked him up, and it seems possible that he has a net worth of $300 million, enough to let him do the altruistic work of government and building without distracting anxiety.

Or rebuilding? I cannot estimate and I hardly know how to research what it would cost to redo San Francisco and the Bay Area (in a state where Los Angeles needs to be recovered, too, along with all those poppy dots we saw in the Caltech map). In San Francisco, we are talking about the Golden Gate Bridge, which cost $35 million in the mid-1930s. And surely the Bay Bridge was devastated, too. That cost $6.4 billion when its new version was opened in 2013—though that was only half the bridge.

We will need a fresh downtown. (Let's see whether we can avoid homelessness and assure affordable homes in the new deal.) And we will have to refurbish or re-create those rows of Victorian residences that are the elegance of the city.

The whole thing, the entire enterprise? In 2018, the value of San Francisco residential real estate was put at $1.3 trillion. And commercial . . . ?

Or maybe someone, Mr. Mnuchin or his boss, says, "Well, honestly, it's not practical, not the sort of thing a very stable genius would undertake when anyone can see that the same upheaval could very well happen again." So let California go empty and idle? Wasn't its plan always a reckless gamble, trying to defy the laws of nature?

Don't most Californians always ask "What in hell am I doing here?" in the aftershocks that follow a big one?

It's the aftershocks that really get you. In the week following Loma Prieta, there were twenty aftershocks of at least 4.0 and thousands that were smaller. We could count them as baby Nicholas went from thirteen, fourteen, fifteen days old . . . as he lay beside us.

Decades later, I find this in my reading: "Kutuzov, like all old people, slept little at night." He is the Russian general in *War and Peace*, the commander who withdraws after Borodino, lets Napoleon enter Moscow, then waits as winter comes for the inevitable French retreat, and follows them, harrying at their flanks. But knowing that the great French sea, *l'armée*, is bound to change course. Still, as he thinks about this, he cannot sleep. So many of us count armies in the night.

And the Rock, Dwayne Johnson, allowed in April 2021 that he might consider running for president.

VAG

In the fatuous but cynical Mnuchian optimism that concludes *San Andreas*, every citizen of San Francisco left uncrushed, unsmithereened, and disinfected is going to be OK. In just a year or two, they will be rebounded, rehoused, servicing robots, and eating a silicon croissant in happiness. "I left my virtual ID in San Francisco," they'll sing in eternal karaoke with the 107-year-old Tony Bennett. Think of it as the future, or normalcy renewed.

Then for the sake of argument, imagine that one wracked body and disturbed soul did totter away from the damage and became "vag," or "Vag," the enduring Vagrant in America, not just the homeless discard, the immigrant, the other, the black, or the Black. I am thinking of the hapless loner John Dos Passos wrote about in *U.S.A.*, the archetype who did not match up to the exacting standards of American competition.

There were three novels that became *U.S.A.* and Vag is in the third book, *The Big Money*, published in 1936, when Laurel & Hardy were still model hobos for America, nearly erased, but uncomplaining and not founding members of an anarchist or communist or terrorist movement mad as hell and not going to take it anymore. The boys were pilgrims still, in *The Music Box*, in their dungarees and silly hats. But there is a moment when Ollie steps on a nail in a plank and we realize that he wears no socks, in shoes that are coming apart. Remember, those boys have gone into business on just $3.80.

It's apparent that America had had some lone walkers since its beginnings, pioneers who might collapse and starve on the prairie, or freeze in the mountains: the nation was built on these unburied bodies. When a rider appears at the start of his epic, in 1889 Wyoming Territory, he is a lone figure coming out of the distance. In the movie, he has his buckskins, his guns, and the calm gaze of Alan Ladd. He is *Shane*, and he has a horse—that animal really was a vehicle and more important than the gun. At the end of the story, he rides away; he has no other name and no apparent money; can he feed himself and the horse on this romance?

By the 1930s, that loner had become a civic figure, casting a shadow of shame or horror on the rest of us. In our obsession with being OK, Vag was easily assessed as an outlaw, or a madman. Try walking across a desert; you may end up crazy, as well as a burden on the community, or someone that community would prefer not to think about.

Dos Passos knew the guy was homeless, and likely hopeless, hesitating between passivity and violence. As a writer and an American he could not deny the faded nobility of this picturesque figure. Vag's solitariness was existential, like the edginess of lonely people in dead rooms in Edward Hopper paintings. This is how Dos Passos described him:

"The young man awaits on the side of the road; the plane has gone; thumb moves in a small arc when a car tears hissing past. Eyes seek the driver's eyes. A hundred miles down the road. Head swims, belly tightens. Wants crawl over his skin like ants; went to school, books said opportunity, ads promised speed, own your home, shine bigger than your neighbor. The radiocrooner whispered girls, ghosts of platinum girls coaxed from the screen. Millions in winnings were chalked up on the boards in the offices, paychecks were for hands willing to work; the cleared desk of an executive with three telephones on it; waits with swimming head, needs knot the belly, idle hands numb, beside the speeding traffic.

"A hundred miles down the road."

That signpost figure is common in the '30s, with different shades of charm. He was a failure or a misfit, a product of disaster, but in such a sea of others there was scant room for pathos. They could not all be Chaplin's tramp walking the infinite empty highway, and as rich as Charlie in life. They might be closer to the guy played by Paul Muni in *I Am a Fugitive from a Chain Gang* (1932), an ordinary decent man who had bad luck and ended up in the worst prison, who escaped and got a good new American life, and was then informed on and sent back to jail—do not pass GO, do not collect $200—so that he breaks out again and lives in the shadows. And when he snatches a brief meeting with his old girlfriend and she asks, "How do you live?" he tells her, "I steal," before he vanishes again. Vag is also Henry Fonda's Tom Joad, with his loose-kneed walk, out of prison and searching for his old home in Oklahoma, at the start of *The Grapes of Wrath.* And he's Robert Johnson at the crossroads.

Come closer up to now, and he could be the Edward Norton character in Spike Lee's *The 25th Hour,* who dreams of evading his prison sentence by going off into the drab emptiness of America; or Harry Dean Stanton, catatonic and stunned, striding across the desert at the start of *Paris, Texas,* wearing a red cap and the unutterable grief of tragedy. Or it could be the guy who has been sleeping three nights on the sidewalk of your own nice suburban street so that you are wondering if someone will call the police—or are they the "social services" now?

If it helps your feeling for community, you can say that Vag is mentally disturbed (instead of outraged by poverty). He came back from Afghanistan, Iraq, or Vietnam (America does geography) deranged by what he had participated in and someday, in Haverhill, Massachusetts, Visalia, California, or wherever, it is possible that he is going to put the one bullet he has always kept in his head. So he is not well, not a helpless visionary or a poet, not assigned in a reliable family situation, not susceptible to employment. He may have been in prison, though now he finds the loneliness of the road is a kind of imprisonment that needs no cell, locks, or solitary confinement. So Vag walks on, begging, stealing, or finding a quarter or a tattered *Tender Is the Night* in the gutter. He has no credit cards, no Social Security number, no ID. He is off the record or the grid. When the stimulus package came through, he was not there.

I realize there was a moment—in the late '60s?—when Vag shifted in our sleep from being a lost pilgrim, or a spirit we had mislaid, to a kind of threat waiting for our breakdown, a hitch-hiker not to pick up. The road in America is one of the country's intense beauties, but somehow fear took it over.

He could be you or me—someday soon we all will be together, wait and see—and not only if the big one scourges the Bay Area and leaves the idea of recovery as drab and hollow as presidential responsibility. The lasting lesson of Donald Trump was how to walk alone in glib improv insanity, as if the desolation of the prairie contained *a road* that only he could see to tread.

One of the most depleting things about the pandemic was the hatred it engendered for Trump. This was the illness so many of us contracted. Thus at a time when we needed to be benevolent, far-sighted, and tolerant (as well as poor), the drive for revenge took away the air. We could not breathe because of him.

But a day may come when he'll be on the road, a scarecrow, with bonespur thumbs. And none of us will slow or pick him up.

We won't even see him. Until we catch his wavering shape in the rearview mirror. Or is it a crow in the car, indignant and ready to kill?

FILE UNDER "END OF THE WORLD"

In 2019, contemplating this book—the research in 2019, the writing in 2020 (such a daft tidy plan)—I was keeping a journal as a growing file of stories and pictures clipped from the media. Day after day, I found myself cutting the *New York Times* to shreds because so many stories were describing calamity. Many of these reports were full of measured reticence in 2019, but there was a running theme: that weather would drown us and burn us. I lost count of how many times "last chance for survival" had been used.

"The paper's unreadable!" complained my wife, Lucy. "It's a disaster!" She was glaring at me through the holes in the pages. I tried to smile. We could still muster the act of being "philosophical" about it all.

There are aching years in our history, cusps like 1914 and 1939, when some people woke up in summer freshness and asked themselves, "Is this the end—the beginning of the end?" That's when our smile ices over. Isn't it in the essence of the human condition to know that our momentum is going to trail away? So that a habit of romance attaches itself to the last moments? Like the way Bonnie and Clyde gaze at each other in rapture before the disruptive bullets reach them. That was 1934 in rural Louisiana, after they had had a spree based on *not* being vagrants.

There is no defense against disaster, no repair—the human race has always been pursued by its anxiety and the rumor of death, straining to keep ahead. Is that why it is called a race?

Our one provision against catastrophe and the cataclysm is to reassess it as a genre. As fun and magic, and as lovely as Warren Beatty and Faye Dunaway. Thus anxiety can be aestheticized.

In 1965, in an essay for *Commentary*, "The Imagination of Disaster," Susan Sontag wrote:

"For we live under continual threat of two equally fearful, but seemingly opposed, destinies: unremitting banality and inconceivable terror. It is fantasy, served out in large rations by the popular arts, which allows most people to cope with these twin specters. For one job that fantasy can do is lift us out of the unbearably humdrum and to distract us from terrors, real or anticipated—by an escape into exotic dangerous situations which have last-minute happy endings."

Fifty years later, *San Andreas* was made to that recipe, with all the technological advantages that had accrued. But as in 1965, the lush display of fantasy was enough to cover over the need for politics and philosophy. A journal can seem like daily fun and sport, but you are writing notes for an analysis of your time.

At the pulpy cul-de-sac of our culture, this accounts for the rites of Halloween, for entertainments like *San Andreas*, the occasions at which anxiety is commodified, and the fear of fear turns camp. This oozing apprehension knows few limits now, as fear turns into **fear.** Or does your taste reach as far as *TERROR?*

Do you need Bernard Herrmann's shrill strings to get the point? Is that how the knife went into that dear Marion Crane of ours in *Psycho?* Is that why we're so crazy about murder and ready to turn it into redrum?

!

Can you cast yourself back to a "before," on the other side of Covid? Can't you see how, in your head, you were already keeping a diary or a modern history, because you guessed things might not turn out well? You could attribute that to "climate change," or its assumption that the weather might alter but we would stay fatally the same, and stupid with it. Wasn't it the case, so far, that everyone who had lived on Earth had died?

As of my arbitrary *"today," April 24, 2020,* the death toll from Covid-19 in the United States has passed fifty thousand. (A year later, it would be ten times that number.) Whereas, in several years in the late '60s and early '70s, the war in Vietnam—a legendary modern disgrace—killed 57,000. Or was it 58,000?

Was Vietnam a disaster or a mistake? It seems that only the Vietnamese should answer that, and they do note that the combat that began with the Japanese and then the French led to the unification and independence of their country. So was that nation-building? Can we see that "disaster" has perils not just for life and decency but in the spread of ambiguity and confusion? There were *Disasters of War* once—but do you know when or where? Did this title come from the person who created the entity, or was it public relations? I mean the series of drawings by Francisco Goya from the period 1810–20 that he wanted to call *Fatales consequencias de la sangrienta guerra en España con Buonaparte, Y otros caprichos enfáticos.* Is the punchier *Disasters of War* part of an attempt by the Prado in Madrid to sell the series?

These are etched drawings to memorialize the Spanish monarchy's repression of revolt and then the everyday catastrophes of the Peninsular War, as the French tried to defeat the British in Spain. While he did this work, Goya was official painter to the Spanish court, so he made the etchings secretly, to avoid displeasing his masters, or the polite society that liked to go to art galleries and see themselves on the wall in good clothes and a respectful light. Or no clothes (remember the naked maja), but in becoming nakedness.

Goya was compromised, smothering his deeper political opinions to get his work done. "Compromise" is often a bad word in artistic commentary, but any honest person knows its pressure. Shostakovich lived many years on the brink of favor and disfavor with Stalin, and he wanted to keep working long enough to deliver the tragic dismay and outrage of his Tenth Symphony, which premiered in December 1953, months after the death of Stalin.

Goya painted royal and social portraits to satisfy the sitters, and he did his *Disasters*. The books say that he had witnessed many of the scenes he depicted. Not that he drew in front of them or as some subjects perished. Grant him that tact, and remember the complicated etching process that he used. Even so, the *Disasters* were not properly seen until the 1860s.

As late as the 1960s, the drawings were kept in the basement of the Prado, as if there was something unwholesome about them. That estimate is correct: they are a savage yet cool or reflective catalogue of indecencies, done graphically yet naturalistically, only occasionally yielding to nightmare, very hard to bear, but harder to avoid. They are a landmark still in the depiction of such disasters and how we should look at them. Of course, they were done less than twenty years before photography, and so I think they are a last triumph in our contemplating the truth of appalling things.

Try this approach to that idea: *On October 31, 2019*, the front page of the *New York Times* had a very beautiful picture, taken by Jim Wilson for the paper. It was of a stricken tree in Sonoma County in northern California, seen at night, with the dead limbs of the tree lit up by sparks or strands of phosphorescent fire that trailed off into the darkness and looked like luminous nervous systems.

This was one tree, but trees are sacred, so that in being dead but aglow this tree was an emblem of the urge of winds that can make fire come and come again, so that even burned-out landscapes—the charred firescapes—are rekindled. On the 30th, in the *San Francisco Chronicle*, there was a matching story about a family who had been burned out in the Paradise fire of 2018 and who now were victims again, cramming replacement essentials in their car one more time in order to find the last safe road away from Butte County towards the south and the city, San Francisco.

When I wrote "very beautiful" I was trying for an honest response and I was not mocking the photographer. We cannot expect a *Times* camera person to wait in the core of an inferno to get the inside truth. Despite such dedication, the camera may melt. If such a picture did survive in a camera that came through the fire, I don't think the *Times* would print it any more than Werner Herzog, say, showed us the desperate footage of the fatal bear attack on Timothy Treadwell and Amie Huguenard in *Grizzly Man* (2005). There are tests of taste to uphold, and beauty can begin in those cracks like a wildflower in a bomb site.

In disaster, there are many anomalies. In 1963, do you recall, at the close of Alfred Hitchcock's mysterious apocalyptic film, *The Birds*, the Brenner home in Bodega Bay stood as a nesting house for all sorts of avians as they watched the silent family get in their car to drive away to safety? In 1963, the connoisseurs of Hitchcock, the numb poet of anxiety, wondered what this ending was meant to mean. Would the gulls, the finches, the woodpeckers, and even crows settle for control of Sonoma County in the game of Risk? Or were they waiting to link up with massed pterodactyl squads from the south?

The Birds had something rare in Hitchcock—an open ending. The film's family story (the question of whether Mitch would be with Melanie) is abandoned in just the way the Brenners quit their home. Of course, birds seem somewhat minor in the scales of disaster. Even if there are about 300 billion birds on Earth. Perhaps all they need is a leader. (The final attack could throw thirty-five birds at every one of us—beaks and hatred—with a few billion left to write the history, and collect the bones.)

In Hitchcock's withdrawal he seems to indicate that he does not know. But in 1963 (so long ago) he could command the crude cinematic technology that let the birds gather and attack. The result is still very frightening. When the birds home in on Melanie in the attic, we are watching a disturbing personal collapse that is movie beautiful.

Tippi Hedren (as Melanie) was actually struck by birds, and bitten, the birds that Hitch was having thrown at her. We flinched, better believe it, but there is something more gaunt in her eyes, and a touch more than her acting was capable of. If one gull had pecked at Tippi's eye, and pierced it, Hitch would never have used that shot. But the threat is essential to our scene. There is a point at which photography often hesitates over its access to horror or the attempt to stay lovely.

I know the homily—a picture is worth a thousand words—and I am historically attached to the culture of the image. But I worry over what it has done to us. I keep wondering whether the photograph didn't slip subterfuge in with all its bluster about

truth—the truth twenty-four times a second was Jean-Luc Godard's pious boast about what he was doing, and a code he ignored.

And surely we are right, and ourselves, in wanting the truth.
In the same Halloween season as it ran the picture of the burning tree, the *Times* had an essay by Samantha Power (once U.S.
ambassador to the United Nations) on the belated acknowledg-
ment of the Armenian genocide that began in 1915. For the
House of Representatives (not without other business) had voted
405 to 11 to say, yes, indeed, in 1915 the Ottoman Empire (here
is the language of genre) had embarked on a campaign of racial
extermination against Armenians (1.5 million casualties—an astonishing number, like 300 billion birds). This was "genocide"
before that word was known (it seems to have been coined by a
lawyer, Rafael Lemkin, in 1943). So now that event had become
official history, and the *Times* had a few old photographs that the
modern eye passes over. Sooner or later, disaster turns historical,
and in that light the energy for fresh depredations may feel freer.
We care about the Armenians, but I doubt I could get your attention for, say, the slaughter of many Mongolians in the thir-
teenth century—indeed, I'm making that up. Or I think I am.

The wealth of omens overflows so that the scale of disasters
can turn gleefully topsy-turvy. How can we measure one mishap
against another? How does the *Times* determine which stories
rate the front page? No wonder then if it turns to the ominous
radiance—for fire is lovely, too—of Jim Wilson's portrait of an
agonized but liberated exploding tree.

Elsewhere, the *Times* noted that there were 1.5 million Kashmiri children kept from school by political unrest. That ran side by side with observations on the difficulty Joe Biden was having on the campaign trail in saying exactly what he or anyone might mean. He had said, "People are being killed in western, in eastern Afghan—excuse me, in eastern uh, Ukraine. . . ." We may guess what he wanted to mean, and we may recognize how a decent man edging up on seventy-seven may get his filing system on "catastrophe" muddled, jostled by the fear that maybe it is too late for his leadership. And because he is upset by the things that will not stay tidily filed. We are all hoping to seem in charge of our storming montage.

In the same days, Thomas Friedman had reprinted in the *Times* an exchange between Alexandria Ocasio-Cortez and Mark Zuckerberg in which the proprietor of Facebook dodged questions about a critical review of false posts so long as they were earning revenue for Facebook and himself. Since Facebook was still the most extensive media platform on Earth (with 2.3 billion users in a month), this too deserved consideration as a disaster in the run-up to an election corrupted and endangered by the president's addiction to lying and the undermining of reporting. Much of which has been accomplished in just a few years, as if to say that our "hallowed traditions" might be a mere piñata.

Still, there was room for one more "disaster"—my antennae were tuned to pick up the word, whether it referred to a dropped pass on a playing field or the concerted legal indifference of the Boeing board on what it had known when, and which it had trained itself to overlook.

So I bumped into one more "disaster." I was part of a panel at Stanford discussing the Alfred Hayes novella *My Face for the World to See* (published in 1958). This book involves a seasoned screenwriter, a success who despises his own work, and a would-be actress, a failure according to the unforgiving standards of Hollywood and its code of a new star being always born and discarded. He rescues her from a muddled, indecisive suicide attempt. They become lovers, indecisively, for love or sex are not much felt in the nearly obligatory alliance or conjunction they fall into. But there is intercourse (a common word for it in 1958). The man says:

"I thought at that moment of Baudelaire's poem: how love, from its shadowy retreat, bent his fatal bow. The arrows were crime, horror, folly. But, ah—it was only a girl, somewhat unhappy, here on an inexpensive rug before a small fire. We exaggerated, Baudelaire and I. Sexual disaster was only the invention of our reluctance, of our own inverted natures. She was only a girl, and expected something: a simple something, the conclusion of a moment like this, the kiss that followed intimate silence, the love-making that went with the loneliness after dinner."

There you are, a single kiss in Los Angeles; nothing to match the withdrawal of kissability in so many Angeleno Covidians in 2020, or the fear of touching strangers. Impulsive love affairs are likely down now, though no one has the cold heart to do the counting. But Alfred Hayes justifies the word "disaster" because he makes this unnamed, undistinguished couple feel like woeful astronauts on the edge of their infinite space.

Not long after reading the Hayes novella, I encountered John Williams's novel *Stoner*, a greater work, I think. It is the life story of a crushed man, William Stoner, a university teacher in English, a man beset with disappointments and dismay, like a Bartleby who feels powerless to oppose those failures. But he gets some relief: a love affair late in life, described with sudden feeling for the body and its waving in hope's wind. "Disaster" isn't mentioned; there is no need for that. But the lovers decide to separate because the world is too hostile to their amour. In a way I seldom find in reading, I cried out "Oh no!" when Williams made this clear, as if he and his characters were making the same catastrophic mistake. But it is in the calmness of that book that its readers have to accept human error and recognize that it is more profound than disaster or triumph.

You know the uneasiness now in opening up the paper—you know there is a war going on in which most of us are clenched against the anxiety and the fatigue of being alive. There's a way in which we beg this tension to end; it's part of the banal (using Sontag's word, picked up from Hannah Arendt) overcast that somehow expects and waits for the end of everything. There was a time when nuclear Armageddon was vibrant in the mind's eye. Our obliteration was so urgent because it had just arrived. So the Cuba crisis in the fall of 1962 was as inevitable as the release of the Bomb in 1945 when it was still only a bomb. But we mature: by today we take the end of the world for granted, or even as a relief.

The big one will come someday. A Richter 10 beckons us like

the four-minute mile or a marathon under two hours. Seismologists say this *must* come; it cannot be escaped in the long-term equation of centuries and tectonic plates. So we say to ourselves, let's take a chance, let's gamble with the numbers—what else are numbers for? We are playing the game that says: perhaps we can have a good time before the darkness and the bang. Don't be ashamed of that: isn't there a pervasive fatalism now that says, I know the world is ending, so I'm going to have a good time while I can?

Don't be shocked, don't look away from the thought. Isn't it what all of us have ever done once we appreciated that we were going to die? Isn't that gaming instinct the foundation of human rationales now, hurried on by the collective realization that God and eternity's moral scheme were for the birds? No wonder those species turned resentful and huffy.

Between Halloween and Thanksgiving in 2019 (aren't those festivals emblematic of the gambler's insouciance and our crackpot fondness for scenario?), I found so many other disaster possibilities. From India came reports—with video scenes on my phone—of crowds gathering in an afternoon smog that had gone beyond being weather and was like the haze of a plague or a curse. The air in parts of India we were told, was "unbreathable." What had caused this? On offer was the mounting exhaust of motor vehicles in a country excited to be getting its first cars, so that people were being ordered to drive only every other day. There was the atmosphere of so many new factories in the most populous country on Earth. There were the fires being set in the nearby farming country, where barefoot peasants did as they had always done and set light to the stubble of one season before they would plant anew.

And in the collection of causal factors there was always the notion, the faith, that "global warming" was adding to all of this in its casual but implacable way—just as faith underlies existence. There was a mood, like the suspense of being with a horror movie. A resident of suburban Delhi told CNN, "Life in the smog is very strange. Many people have a persistent dry cough and itchy eyes. Everything is hazy, so the eyes don't focus on objects in the distance. Everything looks morose."

There is coughing in Delhi, for its 16.7 million people. The average high temperature was only 82 degrees and on cool days it could sink to 55. There might be half an inch of rain in November.

I looked this up and as I did so, I was reminded. . . . As recently as July I had clipped a story from the paper. It was an essay by Meera Subramanian, "India's Terrifying Water Crisis."

Maybe you have forgotten this: there is so much doom to keep up with. So let me take you back *to July:*

"India's water crisis offers a striking reminder of how climate change is rapidly morphing into a climate emergency. Piped water has run dry in Chennai, the capital of the southern state of Tamil Nadul, and 21 other Indian cities are also facing the specter of 'Day Zero,' when municipal water sources are unable to meet demand.

"In Chennai, a city of eight million on the Bay of Bengal [it was once Madras], half of the annual rainfall comes in the fall monsoon. Last year, the city had 55 percent less rainfall than normal. The monsoon ended early, in December, the skies dried up and Chennai went without rain for 200 days. As winter passed into spring and the temperature rose to 108 degrees, its four water reservoirs turned into puddles of cracked mud."

I researched: in Chennai a slum family may have to depend on 7.9 gallons of water a day. In the USA an average family uses 300 gallons a day.

The *New York Times* has been concerned with India lately and I am impressed with the breadth of its horizon, even if sometimes the coverage feels like a curiously warped version of something from the Travel section, which is normally everyone's favorite, in the mood of, "Oh, I have to get away for the sake of my sanity!" There was a different, rather ambitious scheme of sanity then.

But *on November 26, 2019*, on the front page there was a four-column-wide color picture, taken for the paper by Bryan Denton. It showed a street in Mumbai that was a river or a canal or a sewer. The water came up to the hips of the man who was walking away from the camera, searching for something to search for as an alternative to the devastation. The photograph was helplessly beautiful: one could count the several blue tarpaulin sheets—plastic or fabric—that tried to cover the broken-down houses against the rains that had fallen. There were a few people amid the shattered buildings, and there was some debris floating on the water too far away—you have to get away—to be aromatic or nauseating. The floods were hip deep and on that day in Mumbai the temperature would edge over 90 degrees as the humidity closed in on 70 percent.

The water laps up to our laps, and surely Mr. Denton was standing in that water. It's water a good photographer is going to get into for immediacy, holding his camera dry and aloft. Even if he had not thought of four-column width on the front page, who can blame him for wanting to get a picture that we will call beautiful and devastating, a "knockout"? That's what I said to myself. And evidently the editors decided, slap that picture on the front page, let America face that with its latte and granola.

The photograph has an extended caption: "The Promise and the Pain of India's Rains: Over the last century in India, the number of days with very heavy rains has increased. At the same time, the dry spells in between have gotten longer. Climate change and misguided policies are upending the country's relationship to a precious resource. Above, a flooded street in Mumbai. Page A8."

A8 was the first of four interior pages following up on the picture—it was as if the *Times* has been flooded, and I admire the editors' judgment and the choices and the layout, up until the point where the order and the elegance of those things begins to seem dysfunctional compared with the story being told.

So there is a disconnect, I think, between the calm prose (by Somini Sengupta, the paper's global climate reporter)—describing the new intensity of the rains, the damage from the floods, and the way they have let sewage overflow into the water supply and our laps—and the magnificence of Denton's photography.

For example, there is a picture that spreads over both page A8 and 9, eight columns wide. Let me try to put it in words, no matter that like the *Times* we know that one picture can hold as much as a book.

It is a scene in New Delhi. To the left of the frame in the middle distance we see a row of buildings, apartments, I think, in pastel colors with air conditioners and drying laundry attached to the walls. These are not wealthy buildings, but in the context of the whole picture they could be a kind of haven, a safe place, because they loom above the Barapullah waterway, the living motor of flood. There are piles of debris on its banks, a world you wouldn't want to be in. And then there is the waterway itself, which might seem pretty or peaceful in the right light.

But as you look across the picture, in its right half the action is much closer to the camera. The sudden foreground is a movie effect. For Denton has found (I give him credit for this) a broken wall, with a fractured outlet. There is a man showering in its scatter of water. He is in his twenties, I'd guess, naked but for yellow pants. His left foot is braced against a bank or a piece of concrete, and his hands are massaging the spill of water on his body. His dark hair is drenched, clinging to his head, and the broken forms of some lost building stand above and behind him so that the vagrant water may fall on him.

It is not a picture of immediate distress. The man is lean or trim, but not plainly depleted by hunger. The water has that way familiar from water everywhere of picking up the light so that it's streaming and its droplets shine. At 90 degrees in New Delhi,

such a cold shower might be bracing. Yet it is a telling use of illustration to help us understand the condition of so much life
in New Delhi, Mumbai, and all of India. And this is a country
where drought can be as severe a problem. You don't have to
be religious to see that flood and drought are like plagues that
might descend on a guilty tribe.

But I have a question, and I have to wonder, am I unduly cynical or suspicious, or have I spent too long (like, my life) trying
to assess the integrity of photographs? Is the man in that picture
an ordinary Indian, enduring the difficulties of that very hard
life? Is he a passerby, a clerk going to his job in a phone bank
answering computer service questions from Haverhill or Visalia?
Or is he even an actor, without dialogue, I know, without a backstory, but hired to be in the picture? It's not that I am seeking to
undermine Bryan Denton or the *Times*. I think enlisting a human
figure would be legitimate. The picture doesn't work without
him. But I have come to be mistrustful of this beauty—doesn't
the word begin to be a curse?

I sit at my table contemplating the picture. As I turn its page
I take care not to have the paper dip into my coffee cup. I can
handle these things quite well. But in that maneuver, I do see a
story on page A7, by David Zucchino and Tatima Faizi, on reports
of the systematic rape of boys in Afghanistan. One fourteen-
year-old student had had his teacher ask him for a little favor
in return for not failing him in his exams: it was being taken to
the school library and raped. Somehow the cleansing ideas in the
man's shower in Delhi seems a degree more welcome.

Then on page A10, there are Denton pictures of drought—
they are not as striking, but perhaps dryness is less photogenic
than flood.

It is entirely valuable that the *Times* allowed this much space
to such a subject, and I read the text story all the way through
including the remarks of a woman, Rajeshree Chavan, who had
twice saved the sewing machine vital to her income from being
swept away. But she is angry that local politicians come to her
place only when they want her vote. As to any real help for the
climatic problem, they stay away, or in those places in Delhi and
Mumbai where it is possible to find a decent breakfast.

The *Times* does not say and it has readership still who do not
need the point spelled out, but in America, the land of lattes and
scrambled eggs, the local politicians are every bit as bereft over
climate. Their favored solution is to say there is not really a problem. Those lies come up to our laps.

And the *Times* and its best weather experts know that the
problem is so indifferent to solving that it can lead to a feeling
of futility. So the *Times* is telling us the truth in its journalistic
way. Who can blame the paper or Bryan Denton if they have
settled for something like distance in their presentation? It's
as reasonable as one of those fifteen-miles-away horizon shots of
an atomic test fireball in the Pacific in 1946. All you needed then
was Bikini, smoked glasses, and sufficient removal to feel aroused
by being so close.

There are disasters and disasters and one of them is that people might stop buying the *New York Times*. It is one of the few

ironies that Donald J. Trump could perceive that he had helped keep the paper alive, as crows to peck out his vicious eyes.

◆

One might have that picture framed and put up on your wall as an example, or a warning. It might turn you into a photographer instead of persuading you to save the world by other means. I am referring to that double-page spread: the buildings, the waterway, and the fellow in yellow pants taking a shower. I said it was like a movie still, and that comes from the dramatic juxtaposition of foreground and background, the left and the right sides of the frame. I am not trying to disparage the vision of a good photographer, or the picture's shaping of meaning. If you imagine a slow panning shot, following the waterway from left to right, discovering the man, it could be the first shot of an adventure film, let's call it a comedy in which a homeless person, a vagrant, is going to make good. It might have been a way of starting *Slumdog Millionaire*, an exuberant entertainment, the Best Picture Oscar winner for 2009 and a sweet way of assuring Western viewers that really India need not be so bad. Better that than the story in which the man catches typhoid in the fouled water and dies a bad death, after which his corpse is shipped away by the discreet bureaucracy of India.

That's hardly what we pay our $15 for, and it's not the way a top photographer thinks or sees. The matter of news being "fit to print" is tricky and not meant to stay the second cup of coffee or a warm croissant with your own homemade marmalade.

I'm trying to suggest that a photograph is an arrangement; in possessing a frame, it cannot help but acquire composition. Thus photographers act accordingly: they seek to get a picture that will "work." Bryan Denton and the team at the *Times* can do that with a clear conscience because, more or less, they do want "the vexed state of India to be known and noticed." They like to think that they can do something about the problem.

To be blunt or crude about this, you can contrast Danny Boyle's wry optimism in *Slumdog Millionaire*, with its advertisement for good luck, enterprise, and story making the difference in life, with the social sensibility of Satyajit Ray's Apu trilogy. I mean the films he made in the late 1950s in which we see poor people enduring their hardship and suffering so that we feel we have witnessed the real, sad thing, including the gentle caption, "Well, that is how things are in India, so study the case, let its unsentimental flow pass over you, and be a little wiser, or more human." But don't expect even the most anguished movie to heal the world.

I am reminded of one of the most famous photographs of disaster: *The Falling Soldier* or *Death of a Loyalist Soldier*, taken by Robert Capa in Córdoba in Spain on a battlefield of the Civil War. For the most part, it is a photograph of sky, but in the lower left-hand corner we see a soldier, in white, falling back, collapsing. His rifle is dropping from his hand; his head is turned aside in pain or surprise. He seems to have been shot. This is a known and reprinted photograph, and the stretch of empty sky is not casual or accidental; it places the falling soldier as an emblem of sacrifice. The picture was printed in *Life* and *Picture Post*, and it became a flag almost for the Republican cause in the Civil War. It is valiant, tragic, epic ... you can pick your own words. . . . And it is an example of what photojournalism was coming to mean in the twentieth century.

Of course, it is a study in what we call the spur of the moment, so perhaps it should be looked at quickly, too. The longer you study it, the more suspicion grows. There is no way a photographer could catch the instantaneous impact of a bullet: one shooting is so much faster than the other. Even if Capa had been fixing on this one soldier (was he hoping he would be killed?), it's fanciful to think the eloquent photograph could have emerged just like that, spontaneously. And we do not like to think that Capa was waiting for a death because he has come down to us as a good guy (didn't he love Ingrid Bergman, among others?) and because in history we reckon he was on our side. If we waited long enough, Franco would be passed over.

There's suggestive evidence that the photograph was staged. It was a disaster of war designed for liberal consumption throughout the world. Accept it as propaganda. Why not, when it expressed such urgency for eternity? Many loyalist soldiers were truly shot and killed in Spain. And this fellow is falling back into a small upslope, in eloquent display, in the manner we are used to from movies about war and its deaths. Was it "wrong" of Capa and others to arrange a picture that was true to the general situation and which might stir up desperately needed funds and followers for the Republic? Is it that photography is helplessly fickle, or spurious?

It's late to agonize over such questions, yet it's natural to wonder whether Bryan Denton asked the man in yellow pants if he would take a shower under that broken water pipe. And could he then move just a little to his left and put his bare foot on the bank? It's not that I'm discrediting the two of them. I am only trying to recognize how far we now assume that the photographic record of shocking things, of outrage and disaster, has been arranged and presented just as much as the editorial decisions to run these pictures, and to post a writer and a photographer to Mumbai. Not every paper or television news operation funds such assignments. The *New York Times* does try to maintain a broad horizon in a world that deserves to be reported.

What worries me most is the way the inner subject of photography is its own manipulation or duplicity. If you look at Goya's *Disasters* now, you may have to fight through a curatorial claim that says they are "almost photographic." They are not. They are the work of a draughtsman with a passionate conscience who saw things in life, who lived with his compromise and went away to draw them. The nearness to reality or verisimilitude never interfered with his imaginative integrity and the burden of choice any painter meets. He or she wants to re-create the impact of a reality; the photographer thinks of recording it.

We feel that difference and so we have fallen out of the habit of trust that great painting presents us with. And in beginning to exist in that rumor of fakery, a kind of pornography settles on camerawork, a way of whispering to us not to put our last faith in this vivid trick, where beauty is a game. In that technological process, disaster (like love and death) becomes a genre and a piece of theatre.

Consider the case of Sophie Zawistowski. We think we know her as one of the paragon victims of the Holocaust, a version of Anne Frank grown into a becoming woman. A star part, so that she might be ours. The narrator, Stingo, the would-be writer, will sleep with Sophie after she has told him what happened at Auschwitz.

That horror is happening to Meryl Streep, and from the moment you saw the big scene, in 1982, you guessed the honor that would fall on her, like the film's wan light. No matter the hideous nature of the situation, she was going to get an Oscar, in recognition of her extraordinary creative refinement, like a frilled butterfly of breathtaking beauty. The predicament of the camps crystallized as it had captured this prize. The situation—*Sophie's Choice*—was as emblematic as an operatic aria and representative of the twentieth-century disaster. Of course, horror is there in the film, but not the banality (to remind ourselves of Susan Sontag's recipe).

The movie was an unstoppable venture. William Styron's novel had been forty weeks on the *New York Times* best-seller list in 1979—seven printings in six months, then six more for the Book of the Month club. It was seized upon by Alan J. Pakula, an earnest and intelligent writer-director, a thoughtful, sensitive operator who had once produced *To Kill a Mockingbird*, and then gone on to direct *Klute* and *All the President's Men*. He wanted the Norwegian actress Liv Ullmann for Sophie—she had done such fine work for Ingmar Bergman and Jan Troell. Styron had thought of Ursula Andress, a warning that authors don't always understand the movies. But Meryl Streep wanted it for herself—there's no harm or shame in that, though it teaches us that ambition may be the latent energy in all actors. Somehow she prevailed in the choosing. There is a story that she threw herself at Pakula's feet, as if she was already in an opera. But don't forget Liv Ullmann's face and its constitutional aversion to glamour.

So the film was made, at over two and a half hours, and it was every bit as accomplished as you might have feared. Sophie is "beautiful" in the book; at least she is in the eyes of Stingo, the young writer who tells the story and who has fallen in love with her. It's different on film, where everyone tends to be perfect, or good-looking, or making looking feel good. Streep was movie beautiful for only a few years; it began in *The Deer Hunter* (1978), and she is radiant here as if to match the weight of respect the film is determined to give her. The actress lost a good deal of weight and took on a lot of accent. I do not doubt that she is authentically Polish, but she utters with a meticulous expertise that is almost airless and helps build the mystical, semiaristocratic status of her victimhood. It is all class and calculation; it is a tacit reminder that actors—like the medium of film—cannot help pretending.

Still, as shot by Nestor Almendros, Streep's Sophie is a monument of tragic perfection. Her hallowed face is as fresh as virginity and as old as parchment. It is as moving as Garbo's in so many of her pictures. She looks ideal, and that's the nub of my problem, for her excellence begins to detract from Sophie's situation. In the climactic scene, when an SS doctor presents the choice—she can save one of her two children, only one—there is a sense of her performance or enactment that takes away from something Styron glimpses and scholars of the camps know, that such evil was ordinary, not rescued by drama. Streep is faultless in the scene, but there's the flaw. For Styron knows his woman does stupid things, and I believe Ullmann—a less refined, but more impulsive actor—might have caught that.

In the book, that doctor is plain, drunk, casual: he has old rice grains on the lapel of his tunic. He doesn't really care. But in the picture, a very good actor, Karlheinz Hackl, makes him handsome, icy, very precise, and cruel, so there is a kind of seductiveness in the choice he offers. He is fucking Sophie in his power over her. This is a sway movies are drawn to so often, but which is not felt in the book.

Streep did win the Oscar, and she deserved it. She always deserves it, and usually gets nominated because she commands a strain of brilliant artifice that reassures and impresses the dumb Academy. But the film has its own dankness: neither it nor Pakula was nominated. It did well enough commercially—it is a film we all "know." Pauline Kael was shrewd in detecting its fault line: the postwar romance doesn't fit with the immense wartime story. So the lavish re-creation of nocturnal horror in the camp is like fine embroidery on a shroud, or diamond eyes in a skull. There's the pornography and the feeling I have that this very accomplished and foolishly splendid picture should not have been made. The camps were not an occasion for glorious acting. There is a culture of disaster in that incongruity. It is a way of reconciling horror with attraction—disaster mon amour.

Can we regain the real thing?

Can the unbearable be rendered, or anticipated? Could we not see how India was vulnerable to epidemic?

IN ABERFAN

"Look! I am alive."
JOHN WILLIAMS, *Stoner*

With all the possible disasters crowding in my mind's eye, I re-
solved to be particular. I wanted one clear-cut tragedy, one I had
felt myself. A catastrophe beyond dispute—or so it seemed in
1966.

This is a small event perhaps, by the standard of death counts
and damage, but one that was settled and agreed on—before
forgetfulness set in. There has been too much to remember and
sometimes the diligent obituary purpose feels undermined. You
can look this up, and try to work out how surprised you are, but
a little more than 100 billion people have lived in the history
of our Earth. And died. Not many of them were happy to go,

though some were in relative comfort and mental equilibrium. They were tired; they were ready to stop, to turn the engine off; that's the impression they left with the circle gathered at the end. In Cormac McCarthy's *The Road*, even the boy, the son, admits the wish to die so that he can stop witnessing the road and its dread.

But so many others went badly—so many of us, if I may say so. We were killed and murdered; we were swept away by fire and flood, war and disease. One way or another, we were pursued by the four horsemen of the apocalypse—even if the horses in a peaceful field, those Stubbsian marvels, Houyhnhnms in their colloquy, need not summon up images of Ground Zero. A horse must die, but it is a fine thing, oblivious to a world's closure.

A number of the 100 billion were the victims of what on-lookers would call disaster, and that term ranges from the Black Death to the Great War, the loss of the *Titanic*, and the founding of America. Sometimes it seems as if you have to show some respect for irony or gallows humor in the toll of death.

I have had such a story for years—it lacks taste or tact, but you deserve it by now: a golfer was playing the awkward 11th hole at his country golf course. What made the 11th awkward (apart from its reputation) was a snaking out of bounds line that came up to the narrow fairway as a burn mark in the grass. One day, our player hooked his drive (a hook had always been his tendency) and the ball sailed out of bounds. It landed on a passing road, bounced off the hard surface, and alarmed the driver of a packed motor coach on the way to the seaside. The vehicle swerved.

The driver lost control. The coach went tumbling down a slope and suddenly the careering engine and its load were among a group of schoolchildren having a picnic. There were twenty-two deaths—could have been more, but some of the kids were a hundred yards away playing cricket.

The golfer retreated to the clubhouse. He was shattered, as you may imagine. (I put it that way, according to convention, but it's so hard to inhabit that distress.) There was no consoling him. He sat shaking with his head in his hands, asking the air, "What shall I do?"

Whereupon the club professional, a seasoned Scot who knew of missed money putts and a son lost at sea, sat down beside him and put his firm hand on the wreck's trembling shoulder. "Laddie," he said, "I've told you before. You have to keep your left hand strong and let your right thumb lock over your grip." Something like that. "It's the only thing to do with a hook."

No, it's not a good joke, though it has an inkling about the mad passion called golf. I daresay some sad players would nod and smile over it, without knowing the names or the ages of all the children killed.

I could list the names from Aberfan, and you would nod and say, yes, of course, Welsh names, so alike. But I could show you photographs of the 116 (some of them from their headstones) and we could agree that the kids were prettier than the names, like daffodils growing on a hillside. Or like the columns of the dead printed in the papers during the Great War. About 20,000 British soldiers died on the first day of the Somme, endeavoring to advance at the recommended steady pace called for in the orders. At that rate it would have taken about four minutes to amass 116 casualties. But the British command didn't send children over the top on July 1, 1916, so much as raw, innocent minds.

At about 9:15 on the morning of October 21, 1966, a tip of coal waste slid downhill and swept through Aberfan, a small mining town a few miles south of Merthyr Tydfil in south Wales. The onslaught struck the Pantglas Junior School, where 116 children were smothered and killed. Twenty-eight adults died too.

The horror of drowning in coal slurry. Gaynor Minett was eight; a few years later she recalled, "It was a tremendous rumbling sound and all the school went dead. . . . I could see the black out of the window. I can't remember any more but I woke up to find that a horrible nightmare had just begun in front of my eyes."

There is often rain in south Wales, and it had been heavy for days before the 21st. It was also known locally that there were underground streams beneath the coal tip. The Merthyr Tydfil Borough Council had voiced concern and heard complaints about them since 1944. The regulations of the National Coal Board required that such tips be no higher than twenty feet. But throughout the coal field that advice was ignored. It was the custom and the economy in mining to make several tips close to the entrance of a mine. In October 1966 the crucial tip above Aberfan—tip 7—was about a hundred feet high. It had been growing on the skyline for years, the way so many threats build.

With my son Mathew, I visited Aberfan in June 2019. He

drove us there from his home in Oxford. We stopped a night in Hay-on-Wye. We went to bookstores in that town and had beers on the evening lawn of a hotel. We talked of cricket and Brexit. I asked him about the book he was writing, but he was reluctant to talk about it. That is what cricket is for. He was fifty-four and I was seventy-eight. We live in different countries now. No one has ever meant more to me, but long ago I left him, betrayed him, and we seem unable to talk about the damage that may have done. I think we're both depressed, but perhaps we would have been anyway. I long to mend our feelings before I die, but I think our disaster is obstinate and without solution. It has been our tip.

Next morning, he drove us down to Aberfan, and I believe we both felt in advance that the place would be an emotional test. It is not the easiest place to find now, as if people are wary of going there. There is an easily missed turning off the A470 that circles back to Aberfan. It is in a soft, gentle valley with steep hills above it. There is no colliery now because coal has been reassessed in the British economy. But it's not hard to see what the shape of the place was in 1966. Mathew was nearly two then.

The retreat of coal is not recent, and not even a part of Margaret Thatcher's hostility to mining and the National Union of Miners in the 1980s. Pit closures went back to the 1950s. In 1964, 72,000 people were employed in south Wales mines, but by 1966 that number had fallen by 14,000. Coal mining was under intense pressure to be economical. The local M.P., Stephen Owen Davies (he had been a miner himself and he was eighty-seven), had been worried about tip stability at Aberfan "but had not pushed the issue because of fears among the workers that such a dispute would lead to the closure of the pit." There had been reports on possible removal of the tips and they had been costed at somewhere between £1 and 3.4 million. No action was taken.

In 1966, the population of Aberfan was about 5,000 and most of the males were employed in the colliery, the Merthyr Vale colliery. Tip 7 was being used in 1966; it was added to on the day of the disaster. It was reported as being more than 111 feet high and it consisted of 297,000 cubic yards of spoil and slurry left over from the mining of usable coal. A report in 1964 had been entitled "Danger from Coal Slurry being tipped at the rear of the Pantglas Schools." There were plans for new drainage work, but nothing had happened. The risk was known and buried.

There was a pale sun on our June day in Aberfan, and there were only a few people to be seen on the streets or on the four-mile footpath that leads to Merthyr Tydfil. But I'm not sure how far our own melancholy was a response to the place itself or the imprint of our apprehension on visiting the site of a famous disaster. If we had known nothing of where we were, it might have seemed just an impoverished backwater, a place for hiking or riding, but not a promising place to live. For decades, surely, the black coal tip above the village had been awesome yet forbidding, a thing to close your mind to. Some people felt it looked out of balance. But coal kept people warm in the small-terraced houses of the village, even if it left stains of grime the men could not wash away. But soaked coal dust and slurry is a dead weight, filthy and unwholesome. Imagine being buried in it suddenly. Try conjuring the experience of your own children if they died that way.

Disaster is an outrage for days and years, and many survivors of Aberfan had bad dreams or what was not yet known as post-traumatic stress disorder. That term was unknown then (it came into use in the 1970s), so its sufferers lived in unidentified isolation. But it has become more common or familiar as a label: in the United States now 3.5 percent of the population are placed with it in a year. So it is counted and medicated, but that does not necessarily entail more understanding.

Aberfan is still there, but the grassy hills are growing over the outline of the disaster. The town is only half as crowded as it was. There are two schools, a pub, and houses still. But in other ways it has declined: the chapel where bodies were gathered on the day was abandoned and then it burned down. There are empty buildings and no purchasers in sight. But there is a busy youth center. The river Taff was thick and black once, but it is clear now, with otters and heron. And there is the cemetery, which seems the freshest thing in the town. Or its heart.

What should a community do but put up monuments to its outrage and its suffering? Or simply to the fact that it existed for a future time in which such proof might be in doubt?

As news of the disaster was taken in, the mayor of Merthyr opened a disaster fund. The nation (and the world) responded and eventually it reached £1.75 million. That sum needs to be multiplied by fifteen to see what it means in modern money. Britain was horrified and deeply moved, and money can be a solace to grief and anger, or an alternative to constructive or prescient action. Had the money been spent on drainage or removal of tip 7 there would have been no need for the fund.

In the old cemetery, the ground was leveled and layered for two rows of white arches of Portland stone. The effect was astonishingly large for the place; the bright stone was an assertion of fidelity and loyalty; some felt it had the air of a Moscow subway station. But the stone weathered badly in the wet Welsh weather, and in 2007 a lot of the work was replaced with white granite. The memorial is impeccably cared for—it is the merciful and respectable reason for visiting Aberfan, to pay one's respects, while simply being there to gauge the sadness might seem morbid.

The nature of memorials is a fascinating adjunct to thinking about disasters. They grow out of a duty to remember—or a fear of forgetting. Deep down in the ground of disasters (as with great happiness) there lurks the suspicion that we are temporary and insignificant. So memorials to great loss are dignified, grand, solemn, and conservative; they would like to retain the lost thing. They tend to feel like a god of history surveying what happened from a sorrowful yet secure height. They aspire to a degree of understanding that rules out the idea of mistake or fault.

They are run by dignitaries, officials, and leaders of society, and they generally aim at monuments that are decided before they reach stone or bronze. They are not often assigned to artists who might make something startling and troubling, or in keeping with the actual 9:15 a.m. event. There is no statue in the hills above Aberfan of two child figures, running, clutching at the air and each other, like trees in a storm, like a silent scream. And the substance of the statues abrasive and glittering as if dipped in coal dust. The politics of the disaster—the theft of children's lives and their sudden loss of breathing—is not dealt with. The arches on the hillside have a grown-up sanctimony, earnest, all alike, and a touch evasive.

Evasion went further. Once the nature of the disaster was clear, Prime Minister Harold Wilson decided to go to Aberfan. He was there by the evening. But the chairman of the National Coal Board, Sir Alfred Robens, did not attend that day. Instead, he was at Guildford to be installed as the first chancellor of the new University of Surrey. Officials at the Coal Board covered up this distraction. A tribunal of inquiry was set up, and it sat for seventy-six days. Robens testified belatedly and declared that the streams beneath the tip were not known to the Board.

The process was another disgrace, but it was part of the overall reluctance to assign blame. The tribunal was angry over the Coal Board prevarication. Finally it was firm in its accusations against the Board and "Ignorance on the part of those charged at all levels with the siting, control and daily management of tips; bungling ineptitude on the part of those who had the duty of supervising and directing them; and failure on the part of those having knowledge of the factors which affect tip safety to communicate that knowledge and to see that it was applied."

A few people were censured. But no higher official, all the way up to Robens, was named or accused, and not one person was punished, fined, or dismissed for what had happened. It was plain that the larger public interest, the welfare of the miners, and the lives of the children, had been abused. But the grave air of disaster was enough, and politics were put to sleep. Robens headed the Coal Board from 1961 to 1971, and in that time the number of pits in Britain declined from 698 to 292. Robens retired from the Board, but he was made a director of the Bank of England and a board member for the *Times* of London. He had been elected an M.P. for a coal constituency in 1945 and served as a shadow minister, but in later life he became a Tory in spirit.

The Coal Board had paid each bereaved family £500. There was not one suit for damages. A disaster can be sustained by the meekness of its victims. Later, £5,000 each was paid out of the emergency fund to families with losses—if they could establish that they had been close to their children. Yes, that was required. There are polite, obsequious disasters, too.

Mathew and I toured the cemetery; he took photographs, as if that was obligatory (or because phones have that function now), or as a way of subduing the unspeakable tragedy, a way of paying respect to respect. We were there on a midweek day, and we hardly spoke to each other in the fluttering light of sun and overcast.

In 1966, at two, Mathew had just had a sister born in May, Rachel. Kate was their elder sister. On July 30, I tossed his several pounds in the air as Geoff Hurst scored England's fourth goal to beat West Germany 4–2 in the final of the World Cup.

It was a happy summer, I think, or that is how I recall it, with Aberfan three months ahead. It was not just that but the Beatles' *Rubber Soul* and a Buddhist monk who set light to himself at the U.S. consulate in Hue in Vietnam. I had known that and remembered it—the scene exists forever (or our fashionable forever) in Ingmar Bergman's film *Persona* as a kind of unhealed wound. But I did not remember, and I doubt I ever knew, that outside Rio de Janeiro, on January 11, 1966, there was rain enough for landslides in which perhaps 1,000 people perished. There was dismay in Rio, so an investigation was set up. But then next year there were rains again, and slides, and maybe 1,700 died that year. These things keep happening. We can't be sure of the numbers. The official report on the Brazilian landslides, by Fred O. Jones, admitted, "No exact count can be made when entire villages are wiped out."

I think that was a polite way of saying that Brazil had not known how many people it had.

Does that mean life was cheaper or less valued then in Brazil than in Merthyr Tydfil? Or am I merely noting a discrepancy in media attention and the fact of where I happened to be? Disaster can be a misstep on an easygoing stroll, or it may pass unnoticed without coverage. I think Mathew and I were affected by seeing Aberfan; I believe we shared a sense of its air of desolation—but we are father and son and so we may have genetic affinities. We drove on through south Wales, over the Severn Bridge to Bristol, where we were to meet Rachel, his sister, her husband, Sean, and their son Isaac.

In Bristol, not sure where we were to meet, but looking for a car park, Mathew seemed tense, and then his car developed trouble. We barely limped into a parking garage when it became clear that his car had a serious transmission problem. Help was called in and it was settled that the vehicle would need to be towed back to Oxford. He was very upset; he is a perfectionist, which meant he went extra silent. A broken car can do that, and maybe Mathew was tense simply because of being with me and wanting the day to be smooth. Sons and fathers have such intricate issues. It may be a hundred years before such matters are put to rest. But that is only a blink in the night.

Whatever, I went to sleep that night my head less full of Aberfan and its 116 than worrying about my son. Without being smart or facetious about it, in great crises we need to keep our thumbs well placed and secure. As if security is our destiny or excuse.

I sometimes imagine that Welsh valley, stilled by Covid for a moment, more desolate or green with less life and industry. Like a battlefield that has slept long enough for wildflowers and tangled grasses to knit it back in place. It was a year or two after Aberfan that Hitler studies were pioneered at a small midwestern college—that is noted in Don DeLillo's *White Noise*. That major is everywhere now, I suspect; we are so busy studying our iniquity. Disaster can be a shape in the ground, like burial waiting for us, and as elegant as a valley.

ONLOOKERISM

We may be grief-stricken, and moved to acts of charity. When we see the results of devastation—in Puerto Rico in 2017, around the Indian Ocean the day after Christmas, 2004 (you can add in your best-remembered natural disaster)—we do what we can to answer the appeal. We pray for them, and for the way the disaster was not us. We send flowers or blankets; we pledge money; we are on the side of the victims and their relatives. This can be the best part of us, and it is a modest spasm in the urge for political reform. If we detect an imbalance in the world—if we appreciate that some have little except poverty and bad luck—then a donation can be a gesture towards relief. The funds may help mend the damage, but the gesture is ointment for our sore consciences. Time and again, disaster asks more testing questions about the structure of our society. In that, there is a secret threat to our security and well-being. It is the decadence in onlookerism.

As we make our gesture, we can't help noticing other come-ons—here is the first line of the Wikipedia "plot" for the movie *World War Z* (2013): "Former UN field agent Gerry Lane, his wife Karin, and their two daughters are in heavy Philadelphia traffic when the city is overrun by Zombies." No one ever said Philly was easy, but Gerry is Brad Pitt so we're in.

As any relief enterprise knows, you have to have some footage to put up on the screen, because that's where moral action occurs. Is that shocking? It's not unreasonable to be shocked in these matters.

The screen is not just the soul of our households but the instrument of our relationship to reality. Which is a way of saying the screen has altered or numbed that relationship.

These screens (a good deal brighter and more vividly textured than anything we find in movie theatres) do have petty mishaps that can seem like disasters, two or three times a week. We should admit how easily they intrude on the apparent onslaughts against order—like the mayhem in *San Andreas*, or the attempt to indicate what happened in *Hiroshima Mon Amour*. I'm talking about silly flaws, but they can drive you to fury. How hard it can be these days to actually see the movie you have paid for on YouTube—you have to fight through the bureaucracy of the platform (and digest the pomposity of "platform"). Then sometimes the picture breaks up or turns into a shattered mosaic of crazed pixels. Least of all, but truly unsettling, there can be dust on the screen, or greasy fingerprints on tonight's pornographic sonata leaving smears on the angel's thigh.

The screen advertises itself as a nifty window, but these technical imperfections make us insane. Haven't you thrown the remote across the room? And had to search for it? Then think of the child at the Pantglas School in 1966 who sees the advancing rush of black slurry—the imminence of death in the morning—and wonders if it is a scratch on her screen. Is that fanciful or surreal? In 2001, very early in the Californian morning, in my office, I saw there was something wrong in New York.

This was September; you know what it was. I came upstairs to where my sons were having breakfast, and turned on the television. We saw the aircraft enter the second tower and Zachary—he was six—asked me what movie this was from. I am not deriding him, or the culture we had arrived at, but I want you to see how far we had appropriated disaster (and tamed it) while telling ourselves this was reality, and we were face to face with it. Instead of distant onlookers.

In 1966, sophisticated "coverage" and its bogus intimacy were in their infancy, even if it could seem unfeeling and cruelly up-to-date. The assassination of President Kennedy, nearly three years earlier, had caught television resources off-guard, or napping—that was the rueful language broadcasters used. It was not just that they had no "good" footage of what had happened in Dallas on November 22. They lacked even a standard obituary reel for the young president, some pictures to throw up on the screen while commentators or experts ruminated over what it all meant.

That sort of stock footage is like a blood transfusion still for our vampiric television. For a couple of years it seems, the same sparse footage of Paul Manafort (striding in and out of court) and Don McGahn (sidling into an elevator) might have been actual and unpredictable instead of automatic figments of conspiracy theories. Television has to fill the screen, and sometimes it is desperate. So personality loops are used over and over again, until we may become entranced but indifferent.

Across the spectrum of TV, in the years after Kennedy's death, networks were busy interviewing leading political figures about eminent colleagues as if they were dead, in order that the networks would have a judicious, insightful level of commentary if they did die. Edward Boyle, a sometime Tory cabinet minister, and a decent, intelligent minister of education, told me how odd it felt to go into a BBC studio, have a little makeup and a good camera angle, and reflect upon the life and time of Harold Macmillan on the assumption that the prime minister from 1957 to 1963 was dead already. (In fact, Macmillan would outlive Boyle by five years.)

This experience had made Boyle uneasy, along with provoking an irrational fear that Macmillan might be listening and compelled to respond to Boyle's testimony. Did the BBC go so far as to ask Supermac to opine from the grave about what he had meant to us? Would that have been stretching the integrity of politics too far? Or was it natural TV?

For Aberfan, the networks quickly sent camera teams to south Wales, and those crews added to the congestion of rescue and recovery. There were stories that photographers had asked children to appear to be crying for a shot. There is a Robert Capa in most camerapeople, so devoted to the theory of crucial moments to do anything to get them. That emotional crowding was borne out in the narrow, steep streets of Aberfan and the spectacle of the slurry that had slashed through life like black vomit.

All over the world, the still photographs of that damage were on the front pages with the name "DISASTER," and journalists quickly realized the benefit of a helicopter to get the money shot from on high. There was no kind of information center in Aberfan pumping out communiques.

Things happened by chance. One little boy, unconscious, was taken out of the debris and put with a row of his dead schoolmates. But then someone noticed that his foot was moving, and he was saved. This sort of lucky accident was familiar to us from the history of story. There are anecdotes about how someone had lain buried beneath corpses in a concentration camp extermination pit, and had waited until nightfall and then struggled through the corpses to make a getaway for several more decades of life. That might be any of us, anticipating a mortuary lineup but wriggling like eels for a few minutes more.

Among the cameras sent by the BBC and every newspaper were some freelancers. One of those was Lord Snowdon, Anthony Armstrong-Jones, the husband of Princess Margaret, a professional and heartfelt photographer. He went on his own to Aberfan on his motorbike, even if his normal subject matter was high society. Moreover, the title given to him at his marriage was a link to Wales. Though born in Belgravia, he had a Welsh grandfather and would be buried in Llanfaglan in 2017 at an abandoned church where his family had a plot.

He took pictures and went back to London. It is likely that he told the royal family about what he had seen. Which brings us to his very photographed sister-in-law.

Elizabeth II was forty in 1966, the mother of four children. She had been "the crown" since 1952, when she was twenty-five. Even then, she was perceived as a patient monument to duty, though she had no idea how that trial would be pursued for over sixty years in times of social change so drastic that three of her children would be divorced and the royal family would become a national theatre, thanks in part to the ongoing television series *The Crown*, which she herself was able to watch (but have no say in), as if duty now had to sip at a dish of cold humiliation. By 2019, the queen was not just the monarch in the United Kingdom; she was the woman on the screen. We do not know how alert or dull that real woman is; we likely never will know; in the same way, she may die in ignorance of herself; perhaps she watches *The Crown* as avidly as any of us because of what she wants to learn.

As far as we can tell, in 1966, Elizabeth II resisted the strong suggestion by Prime Minister Harold Wilson that she go to Aberfan as quickly as possible. It doesn't seem that she was afraid of the encounter. Instead, in *The Crown*, and apparently in that moment, she declined to go because that was not the kind of thing the queen was supposed to do. She was above such ordinariness, not indifferent or cold (as she saw it), but as a presiding figure who should not make real contact with her people, just as they were not supposed to initiate a conversation with her.

That state of mind is a disaster, too, an affliction that a nation and its society willingly or unwittingly undertakes. It does not present itself as blatantly as the corpses of children gathered in a chapel, but disasters can work more slowly and insidiously. The queen's initial impulse to miss Aberfan came from a depleting air of superiority, part of a scheme of official attitude that offered £5,000 in recompense to bereaved parents *if they could prove they had close ties with their drowned children.* The poor are so devious.

Which the community of parents took and swallowed without protest or riot in the streets. The queen was above a display of concern or caring because her obedient citizens had elected that way of thinking. To notice disaster, or to complain, is politics no matter the situation in which people feel they are above, or below, such codes of behavior.

In fact, the queen and her court did feel the edge of public disapproval, or disappointment. So after eight days of tidying up, Elizabeth II went to Aberfan with her husband. She wore a red coat—surely someone had decided on that; it was not the first color one might have thought of, though red is the Welsh color in sporting events. She walked around the town. She saw the substantially cleaned-up school site. She spoke to officials and bereaved parents. And every report said she was "clearly moved," no matter that being clearly moved even by 1966 had passed into the language of acting or performance. Some say she wept;

and no one suggested she had done that for the camera. Still, she did not register as a stricken human being or a mother. To be that common perhaps could have been a step towards abdication, or a more thorough realization that the monarchy needed to go. For the queen's being there, at last, did help promote the assurance that things were still "all right." Or under control.

And in 2019 the fuddled monarchy was still there, even if the political future of the United Kingdom was wavering—the very entity that a queen or a king were appointed to hold in place.

The third season of *The Crown* streamed on Netflix, and episode 3, entitled "Aberfan," began with heavy rains falling on a small town and an ominous sinkhole opening up in a tip. As written by Peter Morgan (the creator of the series) and directed by Benjamin Caron, episode 3 offered a view of the disaster itself, with an approaching torrent of black seen through a school window, the explosive impact, and the devastation, aided and made not just affordable but tasteful by computer-generated imagery. Another small town was used as a stand-in for Aberfan. And there was Olivia Colman, tight-lipped in the red coat. She is a good actress, of course, but pictures of the queen that day show someone younger, prettier, paler, and more daunted. Colman could not help it that she was not Claire Foy from the first two seasons.

There was then a scene, between the queen and Harold Wilson (Jason Watkins), in the course of which Elizabeth admits (or claims) that she found that in all the tragedy at Aberfan she felt nothing. There may be indirect remarks from courtiers (off the record) that she did say or feel some such thing. But the scene is most instructive as a measure of Peter Morgan's creative intent, part of his wish to explain that woman and discredit her institution. We may nurture the thought that Elizabeth Windsor is not quite intelligent or searching enough to seek explanation. It must have occurred to her that she is divine or "other." That is her most viable motivation.

But Peter Morgan, by season 3, was captain on an enormous ship, a television series watched and obsessed over across the world. In the nature of drama, it required that its central character emerge as a compelling sensibility, not a mere placeholder. Can the series carry on, with an older actress beyond Olivia Colman—it would be Imelda Staunton—until it reaches a point of bathos where the old woman passes away while watching herself on television? How can it do that without being a macabre black comedy, a mockery of the helpless Windsors, and a revelation of the bereft state of Britain?

It is pretty for the show's many viewers to decide that the queen is aware and sentient. But then in the same season as number 3 of *The Crown*, the queen's son Prince Andrew gave a television interview, from a fine salon in Buckingham Palace, in which he tried to allay fears and doubts about his involvement with sex offender Jeffrey Epstein and young women that Epstein might have hired for a prince. I am not dragging this in. The interview was widely described as "a disaster," no matter that the queen had approved it, and the court had surely consulted with Andrew even if they hadn't written a script for him. At fifty-nine he looked complacent in his privilege, stupid in his attempt to dismiss suggestive photographs he could not remember and finally in his stupefied effort to put the whole thing down to his habit of behaving honorably.

Andrew seemed taken aback by his own drab impact, just as the queen may have regretted not going to Aberfan promptly, or as the British public and her prime minister Tony Blair would feel that she seemed unduly cool or distant over the final mishap of Princess Diana in 1997. But if you're going to have a royal family, then you may have to live with a lot of things they don't get, or wonder whether the centuries-long disaster of the monarchy does not require a republic or a fuller democracy.

If that sounds too purposeful or doctrinaire, then you can content yourself with knowing that in our timeline of history this British monarchy is just a small wave in a wild ocean. Dinosaurs existed for maybe 150 million years and they never knew their T was Rex.

But the House of Windsor took another blow just as the queen was broadcasting to her Covidian people urging, "Never give up." Her younger grandson, Prince Harry, and his recent wife, Meghan Markle, elected to withdraw from their royal duties, in part because they were being hounded and exploited by the British media. It began to dawn on the people just what a liability was waiting on the British monarchy. It was nothing personal; but the queen, that steady old lady, without too much in the way of personality, was holding together an archaic institution with forgotten relevance. Defenders of the royal family used to say how good they were for "tourism"—notional money amounts were cited. Few appreciated that the monarchy had reduced the British public to the status of tourists—while in their own country.

There were too many disasters in prospect in the fall of 2019, and it was curious that a reenacted Aberfan was the prompt for a belated attempt to grasp the nature of disaster and its helpless feeding of our media. But the queen's anguished murmur—that she had felt nothing—hung over the show and all of us. In the media, on the screen, the trick of invention is to revive the old verity of actuality. But in the spring of 2020, as we were gripped by the screening theatrics of disaster, perhaps the human race, desperate for survival, was most moved by the way those who had drowned in coal slurry were not us—not me.

As anyone in the news business knows, the audience swells with the scale of disaster. We are greedy and agog for the discovery that, unfairly or not, for the moment, we have survived. It is not just that disaster befalls other people—it is vital that we are watching their bad luck. We are citizens as onlookers.

ALL THE NEWS

The morning has toast, marmalade, and that first shock of coffee, weird emblems of England and Brazil. This reminds me of the quarterfinal in Mexico in 1970, Pelé and Bobby Moore arm in arm, 1–0 to Brazil, what a game! Mathew was five and I ask him now does he remember seeing the match on television. He says he can't exactly recall it, but he has been told ever since that he did see it. Did it happen, or do I only believe in it?

These breakfast fragments may pierce the lofty overcast in which we cling to ideas of order. There is anxiety afresh now in keeping up with the opposite of order. On the eve of some comprehensive disaster—no mere tremors or waves—I go to the front door and there it is on the stoop, in blue plastic against the rain or just to proclaim, "Look, the *New York Times*." Unless it won't be there one day. Unless the lines of communication and community could be severed.

Do you see that vagrant sleeping on the sidewalk across the street? Did he filch the paper to find out what David Brooks is thinking?

I bring the paper in, freeing it from the blue plastic, and then wash my hands, the first such treatment of the day, and the most assiduous. All the news that is safe to hold?

Since 1896, the left-hand edge of the *Times* banner has said, "All the News That's Fit to Print," but as the decades and the outrages pass, this standard becomes more enigmatic or provocative.

All asks so much of itself. It's an infinity, every day, as vast as the depth of space. It includes the numbers vanquished at Auschwitz, as well as the pretty flowers growing in the commandant's garden. It could require that somehow an ordinary daily paper mention that at breakfast an author had thought of Bobby Moore and Pelé, and then sought out imagery of that game on his phone. More reasonably the paper might have reported that as Mr. Biden denied all interference with Tara Reade on MSNBC, Joe could have whispered to himself, "Cross my fingers."

All is beyond reason and a newspaper light enough to hold. But doesn't the rest of the motto admit that there will be things beyond the net of All—because they are lewd and indecent; because they blurt away state secrets and the necessary security of mankind; because they could expose the newspaper to legal challenge? Or because they are trivial, boring, and as commonplace as marmalade or clocks, and lovers not going off together, preferring not to; or because the paper in its self-appointed authority does not even know about them and lacks the words to convey

their secret? That could involve a redwood tumbling down unobserved in some recess of the northern California forest, or a
great belch of methane—an explosion—from beneath the desolate permafrost of Siberia, auguring the end of the world. We
guess such things are happening, unobserved.

So "All" deserves a pinch of salt, but still the *Times*' own legend is instructive in assessing the News and its love affair with
disaster. From the late nineteenth century onwards, as a bur-
geoning literate audience of gossips extended, we have become
obsessed with the News. We need it as much as it needs us, for
it is a business as well as a river coming down from holy mountains of truth. I'm not sure I can think of a graver alarm in the
morning than if the paper was not there on the stoop—and then
twenty minutes later the Internet went out, too, depriving me
of that other daily diet: the sites for CNN, the BBC, and the
Guardian, just to see if there's agreement on how bad things are.
Can you imagine the loneliness of being cut off from the media?
Even when things are not all right, their presence, their on-ness,
tells us our chaos is under consideration or being counted.

It may have been a clear trust at the outset of modern newspapers that there would be good or fit news. And journalism did
its best: it included births and marriages at a suitable social level;
it was eager to say "The War Is Over" or "No One Is Poor Anymore." Perhaps a core of happiness in the papers is the regular
and legitimate pleasure of seeing, "Fisk's homer in 12th wins for
Red Sox, ties Series" for game 6 in the 1975 World Series, Red
Sox against the Reds, another of the greatest games.

So we do our best. I have said sometimes in the *Guardian* or the *New York Times* that this film is so good you *have* to see it. Exhilaration is waiting for you. But the Red Sox lost game 7 in 1975, and England was knocked out of the World Cup in 1970 by West Germany. Every sports fan is fatalistic, and patient with brief success and glory. We know doom is coming.

Surely that dread has seeped through the supposed neutrality of the News. The melodrama has been clarified and insisted on. Modern history has struck an unkind bargain with us, lit up by News. The bad stuff is coming down, and we do expect it. Plain news, amiable, dull news, the calm of uneventfulness, these do not sell. Well-being is all very well, but it's stupefying and it may leave a paper without a page 1. The standards of health in the world have been transformed. The struggle with Covid will be heroic, ingenious, and a glory. We will say we have won. The reach of all levels of medical education has improved. In many parts of the world—call it the known world—poverty has been pushed back. Though this does not apply to the unknown world and the areas judged too backward or deprived to merit news attention. Unless they can become a hot spot.

In 2017, a part of the United States suffered a disaster that stilled life itself. The official casualty figures crept up towards 3,000 after an astonishing natural cataclysm. The physical damage has still not been dealt with. But a president traveled there to offer comfort and paper towels, to be a hero, and wondered aloud wasn't the death toll 17. There are natural disasters and unnatural leaders. The place was Puerto Rico, an unincorporated

American territory, after it had been hit by Hurricane Maria, a category 5 storm, with losses of $91 billion. In turn, FEMA gave the island, that part of the United States, $5.4 billion.

The death count in Puerto Rico in 2017 was suppressed, but as we have learned in 2020 that is an American habit, because while the spectacle of upended houses and collapsed bridges can be a filmic treat, mortuary footage is not welcomed on the News, not when some kind of happy purchase is going to be urged on us every seven and a half minutes in the commercial breaks. There were TV scenes from Puerto Rico, but you may have forgotten the name of the brave mayor of San Juan who mocked and scourged presidential indifference to Puerto Rico and to fact. A disaster on TV quickly turns the media into its accomplice. Three years later, the death toll was admitted as more than 3,000.

But if we confine ourselves to television news, which had become a national habit by the late '50s, the lessons are complicated. A newscast cannot really say that poverty lost a quarter here today but gained a dime there—in part because that progress is not easily visualized as coverage. Or not as much as the medium expanded in the era of assassinations, the unrest brought on by pursuing civil rights, and the daily journal of the Vietnam War. As never before (and never since), the progress, the pain, and the futility of a foreign war were open to enterprising newsreel coverage and brave reporters. The blood and the jungle were red and green. The discipline of security or paranoia had not yet thought to impede journalistic scrutiny. So the audience got a version of the whole thing, interspersed with interviews in which leaders and generals assured us that everything was under control. As if they knew that our comfort and confidence were vital to the nation and the steady bolstering of the newscasts with the commercials that made the production viable.

The economy and the well-being of Puerto Rico had been in tatters before 2017. It was a disaster waiting to be identified. But that condition of neglect was no more reported than the coal tip that waited above Aberfan.

So there were landmarks in television of the 1960s, like Walter Cronkite on CBS telling us that President Kennedy was dead, with a hesitation and a tear that felt entirely natural, and his February 1968 words to camera, "For it seems now more certain than ever that the bloody experience of Vietnam is to end in a stalemate," and the tacit understanding that that verdict was equivalent to a defeat.

Cronkite did not always get the highest viewing figures in America. He was in rivalry with the NBC and ABC networks. But he had an audience in the high 20 millions, and he was sometimes called "the most trusted person in America." In part, that had to do with no one knowing his political allegiances as he honored a broadcasting tradition of objectivity or detachment. This was in a media climate where close to 60 million people were watching nightly news on television when the population of the country was only around 210 million.

Today, those three networks have more competition, but the viewing figures are approximately as follows: CBS, 7.5 million; NBC, 9 million; ABC, 12 million. In total, close to the number

CBS had enjoyed on its own by 1968. But our TV landscape has shifted, so we need to add these numbers for cable newscasts: Fox, 4.1 million; CNN, 2.1 million; MSNBC, 2.4 million. Do you see how many of us have given up the News?

My wife has recommended that I watch less of MSNBC (because it is so upsetting or claustrophobic), but then she settles down to watch with me, arrested by the show's urgent voice. We are members of its church. We know the team: Brian Williams, Lawrence O'Donnell in the evening, with the whole gang in the day—Chris Hayes, Hallie Jackson, Joy Reid, Stephanie Ruhle, Chuck Todd, Ari Melber, Katy Tur, Steve Kornacki, Nicolle Wallace, Ali Velshi. And Rachel.

If you're reading this book (or any book?), you know who Rachel is. She is the La Pasionara or the Joan of Arc of modern television, always in severe, undecorated black, endlessly cheerful even if the material of a report is drawing her towards tears. I don't know that America trusts people on television nowadays, but Rachel Maddow has been a voice and a defiant conscience that has occupied a warning position, close to the heart of liberal America. She is one of the few talking heads we have who insists that we need to be awake. Because she is certain that disaster is at hand. Her unquestioned air of courage depends on a shared feeling that the worst is yet to come—soon. No one watches her to be relaxed.

She would have shocked Cronkite, but we are no longer suckers for his urbane, "That's the way it is," to close a newscast tidily so that we can move on to dinner. Rachel knows "the way" has gone haywire, and while I don't think she drinks (seriously) or despairs, I feel she's asking herself why not. Her hair is short, but she could be tearing it out after the next break. We occasionally hear about her secure private life; she must be materially comfortable. But Walter's "way" is beyond the having now. She knows she's facing disaster, and she's torn between full candor and keeping the show and our spirits pulled together. It's not going too far to say she sometimes seems on the edge of a breakdown (just like her society), and she may be warding that off through the energy and vivacity of her performance. So she acts like someone close to cracking up. That's why watching her is such a strain that Lucy might urge me to take a break.

I hear she gets $7 million a year—over at Fox it is reckoned that Sean Hannity makes four or five times that sum, spinning his on-air salary off in many subsidiary ventures. (Lawrence O'Donnell, who follows Rachel every night, and chats with her like players on the same team, makes $5 million.) But Rachel can't reckon that any contract is going to last as protection. She is terribly trapped. She has a solid unsentimental hunch the world is ending—because we are such shit and greedy fools in a culture of liars. Even if it doesn't end, even if that golden monster of shit is removed and sent to St. Helena or the Farallon Islands to live out his days. Even if Rachel wins in that way (if a Cronkite scheme of winning still lasts), she's in the soup. You see—and here is the tricky point with the News—she depends on disaster.

MSNBC was founded only in 1996, and for several years it trailed Fox and CNN as a cable news station. Rachel Maddow became a fixture at the station in 2008, and as she worked her way to prominence (with less emphasis on glamour or "sexiness" than any talking female head in her field), she was carried on the current of the moment as MSNBC recognized a crisis and a peril coming in the greedy swagger of Donald Trump. There is no question but that her passion, her humor, her research, her timing, and her desperation are because of that man. He brings her to life and sneers at her fake news.

And no one works as hard. She has a staff, of course, but she is herself a fearsome worker who reads everything, who writes a lot of her material, and who has urged herself forward into what amounts to a unique TV monologue, a twenty-minute oration, straight to camera, without too many residual resources or backup, but arguing a case buried quite deep in the past, and rising to charges of neglect, iniquity, and something close to wickedness. No one else on cable news, or on television, talks like this. And Rachel does it with fluency, so it is hard to tell when she is reading a teleprompter script, or simply winging it on the updraft of outrage. She is amazing television and she seems exhilarated sometimes by the power she is unleashing. She could yet get carried away into anger or mania.

On *Friday, May 1*, with Covid-19 deaths going past 64,000, she delivered a report on infection in meatpacking plants across the country—in South Dakota, Nebraska, Iowa, and Minnesota. Those large factories are not open to outside television coverage any more than they are happy owning up to numbers on infection and death among their workers. But Maddow is nailing them, with a repeated film loop from the past of packers in close proximity presiding over a moving production line carrying the cuts of animal flesh, to masked testimony from a few current workers and local police chiefs. The import was damning. The meat plants were revealed as concentrations of infection where the workers could not maintain social distancing and where they were short of protective clothing and tests.

There was more. From her research, Rachel had the record of recommendations from the Centers for Disease Control on how such plants should handle the risk of infection. In its normal practice, the CDC (a federal agency) gives unequivocal instructions to meat factories and all the other businesses that might be pushing the limits of the virus. These prior memos were put up on screen: we could read the firm language. And then within a few days, that tone softened as the CDC suddenly picked up a degree of polite suggestion or accommodation, a code of "if possible" that was gentle on how companies could finesse their problem, and as an attitude that coincided with President Trump ordering the meat factories to reopen, to stay open, to insist that workers show up every day. With or without testing. Whatever.

The thrust of this reporting was to ask, "What has happened at the CDC?" Why has that austere regulatory body, a safeguard and a standard for everyone, turned what Maddow called "mealy mouthed." What had happened to Dr. Robert Redfield, director of the CDC and a sometime member of the Coronavirus Task Force led by Vice President Mike Pence? Rachel Maddow promised there would be more to come on this inquiry, and it has been a feature of her role at MSNBC that she sticks with issues, cases, and potential holes in the boastful system. It has been her policy, "Trust what they do, not what they say." There is an impressive level of persistent journalism at MSNBC that is rare in television news. Cory Gnazzo was executive producer on the Rachel Maddow segment, and he had worked with her for years. Phil Griffin is president of the station.

A night on MSNBC will have talking-head pundits, as well as direct testimony, as in the distraught Zoom stories told by nurses and doctors in New York or in other flashpoints. The show has acquired some firsthand video coverage of the crammed wards with individual faces blurred out. But for the most part, the station is all faces. You can close your eyes and listen to the dire information they are passing out. You will be as moved as Rachel, and you may even say to your room, "I'm as mad as hell and I won't take this any more." MSNBC is hard to watch, and I suspect its faithful viewers cherish that. Every two or three weeks there are people who need a little R&R, like infantrymen coming off patrol in Vietnam or Iraq. But Rachel and the others carry on in a similar sense of bleak duty, and the certainty that their jobs will be done if the news starts getting rosier so that its nightly menu is a horticultural center opening in Des Moines, quintuplets successfully delivered in Amarillo, and LeBron James winning another championship.

But suppose you have your eyes shut still, as Rachel closes one segment with something like, "Don't go away. We'll be right back," in that endless refrain of the anxious medium. Then her woeful ecstatic voice gives way to the dulcet blah of commercials. Several of them are for medicines and for sophisticated responses to cancer, erectile dysfunction, and unsightly blemishes. But then among the ads there comes the sound of desultory, pastel music. Nothing else? Are ads really this shy?

You open your eyes and you are seeing commercials (or suggested promos) for the Centers for Disease Control, spelling out its official function and crushed sensibility. These ads do not say anything about ignoring or denying Rachel's accusations. But neither will she refer to these embedded nullifications when she comes back on camera. We have structural malaises in our media condition that need more direct attention. The News and what it deems fit are vital nagging wounds in our sensibility. And even Rachel Maddow stays silent in the face of them.

◆

On the eve of the 2020 election, Rachel and the others were talking faster and faster, in a mix of exhilaration and dread. They were desperate for the result, but could they think beyond that?

Were they to win on November 3—I am talking about our side—there would be a party period of jubilation. It might easily shade into a grim vengeance sending several people to prison (please list your recommended names with the orange uniform). But the crisis would subside. Would we the onlookers have the stamina for more and more of Rachel—much less her customary relentlessness with a new president and what might be his fumbling of "normalcy." The air could go out of the MSNBC balloon for a year or two, or the rest of time. Our gang could be out of work.

But who could foresee that relaxation in Narcissus Bone Spur? Who could doubt but that in exile—a Napoleonic condition—he could create his own television network, crueler than Fox, where he would rant all day against those who had beaten him and betrayed him. Until, at last, with his poisoned smugness he would look at the camera—at us—and say, "You know, I like this more than being president. I never really wanted that. I just wanted to be on television."

And that is a realm where he is beyond impeachment. Fired from so many other strains of discourse, he could be on TV as much as he always watched that medium—he did resemble the queen following her own decline.

The air of victory for Rachel and MSNBC did not last long. Surely she was smart enough to know that her essence had been lamentation, pain, and attack. How could that energy survive coming to power? How could this kind of television exist without the various sides full of wrath, hatred, and the urge to tear enemies apart? Was it at last a proven case that our news had to be a blood sport, from which we shrank away in increasing fatigue and shock? Was there enough point in winning? Had the news become a show, a theatre, and only theoretical?

PANDEMIA PANDEMONIUM

As well as a plague, you need a journal, a book, and a pen, something mundane to hold the nightmare at bay. Keep composing, until you are persuaded. Many of us have had such ploys at hand. Early on, I promised myself that I would read *War and Peace* again in the crisis, as well as Hemingway's *Death in the Afternoon*. I have kept those large paperbacks on my desk, and had to move them aside to play a little solitaire. In the collective forces of the virus, the diminished economy, our discovered regret over racism, and the vileness of the leader, I have been playing the game I still call patience—that is its English name.

How quickly the early anecdotage of disaster turns into a journal of the plague year. One virtue of that approach is in imagining a future point from which we will look back on the disaster as veterans or mourners. I daresay that most diligent diarists have had the feeling that something bad was coming. This is also a literary model of that experience in the dark before dawn, of waking up and listening to your companion's breathing.

"Are you there? Are you all right?"

Or could the I doing this be alone?

Plenty of old people (like General Kutuzov in 1812) have known the bleak comfort in being still here for another day, even if they are only answering the questions raised in their own sleep: Still here? Still oneself, still alive?

And then getting up to write it down, in the hope for posterity and its printed record. The diarist and the writer nurse some absurd hope for an immense archive, the Ozymandias Papers, that will last and last. Yet the only record or imprint left in the Yucatan from 66 million years ago is the immense displacement and shock in the ground. There were no libraries then in the line of fire, filled with irony and tragedy and the final irony of pathos becoming irrelevant.

So like soldiers in the trenches on the Somme, or Captain Scott dragging a sled towards a base camp too far away for undernourishment—it was eleven miles—we find our presence and our continuity (or the hope for such things) in a daily journal.

March 23, 2020, San Francisco. It seemed a merciful weekend in California. The Sunday was fine and dry; the sun shone, the wind stayed gentle, and shelter-at-home was a week old, like a new game. This was the first holiday in the shutdown in which we were ordered to stay indoors, except for those lifelike activities, like shopping for food, filling the car with gas, and taking exercise. A $2 trillion stimulus package was "in the works," and

Mr. Mnuchin at the Treasury would be working it through. We didn't know yet, but it was his bright idea that the presidential signature—that harsh black brand—would be on the checks. There was so much we didn't know yet.

So Lucy, Zachary, and I shopped for food, six feet apart at Whole Foods, and then we drove to the headlands in Marin and took a walk on the Rodeo Valley trail. It was not crowded, but we were not alone. We passed walkers, bikers, and parents with loaded backpacks of infants. There was calm and amiability in the air. A woman came by on horseback and we stood aside for the warm barrel of its swaying body. We said "Hi" and "Good morning" to strangers, just to make it clear that that could be done still. There was a modest sense of community and adventure, sentimental perhaps, or evading the unquestioned future possibility that in the extremis of survival, with limited resources but ample firearms in our time and place, community and privilege might slip into conflict or contest if poised over the last Chateaubriand and the one remaining bottle of the best pinot noir ever made.

We were walking beneath a long ridge of scrub and trees. From somewhere in that slope and its undergrowth there came a desperate animal scream. Though maybe a hundred yards away, it signaled pain and terror. Zachary thought he saw a dog in the distance, then he felt it was a coyote.

These cries continued, as if the animal was in great distress. Then a young man on a trail bike came along. He believed his dog was loose in the area. He dropped his bike and plunged into the undergrowth. After a few minutes he emerged with his dog on a leash—not a big dog, but seeming fit and strong, and gangbuster exuberant, as if he might have won a victory by attacking a coyote.

Meanwhile, the cries and the calls of the coyote continued, stricken and stationary. Did it have a broken leg or something to stop it moving? As if it had a place to go. Coyotes live and die in these hills. It has been the mounting uneasiness of the City that coyotes are venturing more and more into our areas of residence. There are warning notices posted in the Presidio park where people walk their dogs; we are not to feed or encourage the coyotes. There are anecdotes of them being seen in well-kept gardens and of a coyote loping across the Golden Gate bridge at dawn, as unheeded or nonchalant as infection.

It is up to us to decide whether those stories are proof of the glory of nature, or warning signs of urban order or propriety cracking. I have had similar feelings in Las Vegas, where it is hard to tell whether the bright city is flexing itself to stretch out into the desert or is the patient desert waiting for its eventual victory by attrition or silent faith in itself, deaf to the burbling of all the slots and steak breakfasts.

That was our Sunday outing.

I wonder what happened to the coyote.

We are desperate not to be solitary or alone on the road. I cannot still that urge to touch others I do not know—in the way an epidemiologist would claim to know—but I have heard the horror stories of 1918, and the revenge that Spanish flu took on those who decided to keep their parades and their parties. There is an article in the *New York Times* today by Thomas Friedman that shares my wondering: could the tense grip of isolation shut down the enterprise of community that is as precious and as much ourselves as life and breathing?

After all, it is said that the death rate from our coronavirus is 1 percent of the number infected. In California, that could mean 25,000 deaths. Be more open or careless, skip a decimal point or two—suppose the number is 2,500,000. That seems a prodigious number, but so much less than the 50 million, the estimated worldwide losses in 1918–19, when the population of the world was less than a third of what it is now.

There is dread in such history, not just from the magnitude of the losses, but because we can foresee a time and a culture in which numbers and their sentimental severity direct so many policies. If it is a war, a desperate close-run thing, there is no alternative to refusing to be defeated. There have been battles and wars where generals and leaders, calmly enough despite their distress, organized or countenanced the disposal of such numbers. This is Kutuzovian mathematics in a campaign that probably reduced the French *armée* by 80 percent—say, 400,000 men lost in the mud and the snow. The Russians lost about the same number. We are all, leaders and followers alike, engaged in the regrettable process of removal. But we should be careful to understand that mere survival can terminate the valuable things that make us treasure life. Human beings have not always been here, and there; and will not be—we have no eternal rights on the property. Every owner is renting, or is it squatting? The coyotes and the desert creatures are patient. Persistence is so much in their nature they do not need to be brave or "constructive"—those warm moods are a human fantasy and a way of wanting our consciousness to hold a place of religious authority.

Our consciousness has such variety, and its complexity may be as vital as any of our noted achievements. So it is with disaster (our epic once, but our context now) that it takes such disparate forms. There can be comedy in the range—there should be—but sometimes its apparent insanity or facetiousness demonstrates the depth of our hesitation. In our oceans, we sometimes call those depths abysses.

On *this same 23rd*, there is news that Harvey Weinstein has contracted the coronavirus. And there are reports—like drowning figures in the ocean of reports—that substantial new chunks of Antarctica, the Thwaites Glacier, have fallen away, that the Tokyo Olympic Games are close to being postponed, and that monarch butterflies are never seen now in places where they were once taken for granted.

If you are smiling, stay open to graver data. I just proposed the possibility of the coronavirus taking out 2.5 million of us before the discovery of an effective vaccine. That is a shocking number, not just in its extent but as it towers over the casualties from hurricane Katrina (1,200 plus), 9/11 (2,977) or the Johnstown Flood of 1889 (2,200 plus). It is also 2,500,000 × Me, which likely means some of those close to You, including those younger than You and supposedly in your theoretical care. It is a total getting on towards half the number popularly associated with the Holocaust, an event lasting seven or eight years, whereas the 2.5 million might be delivered in a year or two.

(By the way, we might mention the Indian Ocean tsunami of 2004—do you recall?—epicentered off the west coast of Sumatra but affecting a range of other shores, including Thailand—estimated deaths: 227,898. Maybe you have enough already? Press CONTINUE.)

Look aside, even to a piece in the *Times* from *March* 22 on the 1918 pandemic (as a matter of interest, when I first wrote this I mistyped 1818, then as I corrected it a hunch struck me: I looked it up, and 1818 saw the first heavy onset of a cholera epidemic that killed between 1 and 2 million in India. Press CONTINUE.)

As the *Times* reported, the 1918 pandemic killed 675,000 people in the United States.

The 1918 pandemic now is described as long ago, and even quaint. But I had grandparents who were alive and alert at that time, and parents who were about ten years old. The anecdotes of the Spanish flu are falling away, or they were before this year. That makes us mindful of how the immediacy and horror of Holocaust losses (a number tattooed on all our wrists once) will lessen in the collective consciousness. This is tricky or indelicate. Let me just say that 102 years after 1918, I think we can live with 675,000.

The mathematics are not easy to deal with in the midst of a plague if they are presented suddenly, with vibrato, when too many bodies need to be buried. Therein lie so many of the human and political dilemmas in dealing with disaster. For nothing is so tactless about it as its exposure of the sentimental norms existing in society.

As I write (it is *still March 23*) the United States Congress is in a logjam over what is called a "stimulus package." That label is provocative, for the package is really aimed at some kind of rescue. Even in a famously electronic culture, just two weeks of pandemic emergency have signaled "collapse" in the economy. Thousands of shops, restaurants, and bars, ordered to close, are at a point of bankruptcy. At least 80 percent of the population faces some pressure now of not being able to pay for rent, mortgage, or subsistence groceries. That this crunch has come so swiftly is a mark of how our administration refused to credit or act upon the warnings it had from its own intelligence. It is also some proof that boasts about the economy had papered over widespread vulnerability among Americans. The extent of the crisis (a catastrophe about to occur) is directly attributable to government incompetence. But Donald Trump had been going bust all his business life. Moreover, there is every indication that the United States has not come close to the worst in the decline. I told you at the outset that innocence would be required. The illness has its own destructive power, but the greatest disaster could be in undermining the last spasm of capitalist confidence.

So the package of measures being addressed by Congress (and notably the Republican-led Senate) was to deal with the current injury and to assist the public and our economy to a time when the pandemic might have been tamed enough for us to be waiting for a vaccine with optimism. If you doubt that optimism and marvel at the specious plan for economic transition, if you think it's humbug, then at least you are alive.

Just don't expect to be listened to.

By *Tuesday the 24th*, there is spreading talk that Trump is impatient already to "reopen" the economy. He says it is not natural for America to be closed, and that claim is more historically astute than he can ever know. Suppose in the panicky DNA of all escapees there is a revulsion at being confined. This gets at the most endearing and mysterious philosophies in America, the feeling for human and social nature as expansive and aspiring ideas in which space is a tribute and an inducement to desire. You can read this grandeur in Whitman and Melville, and you can see it in Bierstadt's grandiose landscapes or in Hockney's entranced gaze at the Pearblossom Highway. It is there in the infinities and discord of Charles Ives and the hectic highway improvs of Charlie Parker.

This is Amerikana, and maybe no one will ever know for sure whether its attempt was democratic or fascist, or simply defiant of the innate limits facing mankind. If America was escapism incarnate, it had to be ready to dump every OK'd scheme.

Native tribes were butchered, herded, and stuck in reservations, making the saddest places in America, and forgotten now. As a kid I sentimentalized Crazy Horse for his victory at the Little Bighorn. (Custer seemed a classic golden jerk.) I have sometimes given money to Oglala Lakota College in South Dakota. And I honor the way some Sioux and other nations have "made it" in

America. But I wonder whether that hopelessness and humiliation did not require some ultimate "Indian War" in which the nations had fought to extinction to defend their way of life.

What happened to native America—the way it reshaped the land and the space for adventurers and escapees from Europe, for business, is tragic enough and incriminating. How many of our indigenous people died in oppression—in war, captivity, illness, and poverty? Try 50 million. And are still perishing. We new Americans had to acquire the straight faces, and then the pious sorrow, that could accommodate other people's disaster. But what occurred with slavery is so unequivocal, so radical and lasting, that it tells a more insidious story about our capacity for finessing ruin.

It seems fanciful or evasive to contemplate the inner dynamic of disaster—its poetry as well as its doom—without considering it in the spaciousness and the fierce empty-headed hopes of America. Weren't the nation's insane ambitions destined to crash? This is a country and an idea I chose to come to. But you dare not cross the great empty quarter of the United States without feeling the desperation in "United." You recognize how the experiment spread damage and madness, like putting butter on the land. So it built Hoover Dam and Las Vegas and those clever test sites, to tell nature off. And those gestures had contempt and cruel coldness for Native American culture and its attempt to abide by the emptiness, without being businesslike, and think it might be holy. So out of the majesty of the wild area, we branded it with the assertion of "Four Corners," the nexus of Arizona,

Utah, Colorado, and New Mexico, as if to tell ourselves it was all under control.

But still the ancient, unmade roads made their way across the ground, waiting for vagrants. It is strange: these trails are not always visible or apparent from the ground; but if you are in an aircraft, you can see them as plain as lifelines in your hand.

Slavery is not only American; it was a system and a behavior found in every society; after all, it is a blunt reminder that some people are more hallowed than others. This attitude still oppresses women in the land of the free, where that is explained away as necessary biological assertion—or seductive charisma. But no economy or attitude was more reliant on slavery than freedom-quoting America. Our scholars estimate that in the United States, there were 12.5 million slaves brought in from Africa or the Caribbean. That is a surpassing disaster, yet scholars kept counting—as if playing patience, instead of crying out Great God!

And nowhere else was its aftermath more lasting or dishonest— indeed, we should drop the "after" and let the naked *math* be exposed. That is the disaster we live with, the polite or unruly vagrants we place in the ping-pong of spectators and participants— we are watching black people; they are on a screen, the place we want to be. White people fear and resent black people because of that emblematic casting status. They are givens, pilgrims and victims, and whites are lost souls silently raging at their deprivation.

It is comic, can't you see, but the disaster is inevitable.

I would be astonished if anyone reading this book is not

subscribed to the ethic that slavery was a bad thing, a disaster, a source of shame and guilt. Go to bed without any supper! We are accordingly determined to end racism in America—and yet we cannot doubt the plain fact that, somehow, racism still exists in our land, among those other people we do not approve of. We do not know these people, they do not come to dinner. They are the base, if you like, the reactionaries or the bigots, who still privately adhere to dislike, fear, and avoidance of "colored people." Then ask yourself how often you have people of color in your house "socially"—I have no answer for my own habit. Ah, we say, but things are changing. Yes, they are, but at a pace that could be compared to the effort to restrain global warming. We are not urgent with it, not as desperate or decisive as our ancestors were—three, four, five generations back. Those founding figures have our names and they look like us when it comes to ownership, trading, calm abuse, rape, and even murder.

Yes, I know, you say: I say it myself; and there are those who say we only think we know, because of social distancing. Still, we would like to make amends, and few deny the justice in that. So we rejoiced in the passage of civil rights legislation, and we deplore the earnest policy of suppressing black votes in parts of the Union. We welcome the way black people have taken on valuable roles in our society; we look forward to more of that, though some of us have unspoken anxieties about black households in our backyard out of the need to preserve "property values." Delete the "after" and concentrate on the "math."

We can seem confused, never more so than over the idea of

reparations. Even among liberals, socialists, or radicals there are mixed feelings over reparations, or some redistribution of assets to correct an old worry. This could entail shifts of resources and inventories, the reassignment of homes, jobs, club memberships, or even spouses? It could be a new version of Monopoly. For the most part the word "reparations" is reckoned to refer to money. In practice, that could mean granting $1 to each descendant of slavery, or $1,000, or $1 million. How would you rate or measure a lifetime in servitude?

Discreet objections will come quickly. Such a method of compensation would be "demeaning" to the enterprise of some black people. And so cumbersome. Yet we have lived some time with the scheme called Social Security and its implicit equation of things earned and then repaid. We have not been abashed or muddled by it. We have even come to terms with the way "insecurity" hardly notices the upgrade.

We can justifiably argue that conditions of the soul and the spirit do not translate tidily into checks. Really, we would make that case. We are not well endowed with irony or grace. We shuffle in line with the team élan that esteems checks to suppress the fussy test of spirit.

We could say—I can hear us—that some disasters are beyond our accounting or rescue; they have to abide by time. This case may require a pulpit or the effulgent hypocrisy of someone like Justice Clarence Thomas.

We could say that the devices of social engineering might set back the proper progress of race relations.

We'll say it's unfair. That it won't work. That really it's rotten and naïve and beside the point.

$

Already, *it is March 26*, on another spring day, and numbers keep coming in. So today the count reveals that the one thousandth person has died in the United States from Covid-19. Don't be brave or insouciant about this: don't overlook the idea of 1,000 carried away in the isolation hospitals now insist on. This tragedy is dawning—it may be too obvious in a week—the dramatics of the virus are shifting like the strands of a fertile string of bacteria. We can rest our case on the threat and the evil of the virus, but think of it as a wind, or stirring strings and horns in Shostakovich's Tenth—there is beauty in nature's energy that has no vanity about being called "beautiful."

History insists on a rich vein of irony. Consider the Black Death, or the Great Plague, or the Bubonic Plague—these are all good, intimidating titles. We believe that this pandemic illness was carried by the fleas on rats, coming from Asia to Europe. When this was first suspected, foreign ships were held offshore at Italian ports for a period of forty days—and so we have the word "quarantine."

The consequences were so immense, you have to check the numbers. In the years from 1346 to 1353, the population of the world (say 475 million) fell by 100 million. The illness was hideous: the skin itself turned black and it died so that it could be peeled away. You might have been caressing a breast, and it lifted off in your hand. I know, that's in bad taste, but you see my point.

The plague produced tumors in the groin and the armpits. This yielded to fever and vomiting and death within a few days. Treatments called for drinking wine, letting blood, consuming ground unicorn horn—if you could find a unicorn—and attaching a live chicken to your tumor. I warned you—it was all silly, but these were the most modern treatments in view. Half the population of Paris perished. There was no cure or remedy and no assurance that it would go away or become bored. Every minority in that society was blamed and persecuted because of it. The Jews suffered especially—but you were guessing those massacres.

It is a scene of epic demise, yet it feels as incidental now as hearing about Dutch elm disease in London parks and commons. Clement VI was pope in those years, and he tried to say it was not his responsibility. There was reason to believe that the population of Earth might subside or cease. It seems likely that the number of people in Britain fell from seven million to four million. Geoffrey Chaucer was a child in the time of the Black Death, and he survived to write *The Canterbury Tales*. There are recordings of it being read in a fourteenth-century voice. I think it was that sound that persuaded me into writing:

Whan that Aprill with his shoures soote
The droghte of Marche hath perced to the roote,
And bathed every veyne in swich licour

Of which vertu engendred is the flour . . .
Than longen folk to goon on pilgrimages.

Chaucer's folk were intent on getting to Canterbury, and that is as good a destination as any, but we know by now that our "pilgrimages" are just an idealizing way of taking to the road.

We do not know or memorialize the names of those who succumbed to the Black Death, but that's because we have so meager a sense of the individuality of those years or the culture that believed it was on the cusp of history. As if the Black Death had been sent as a test. But how were we meant to win that test? I put it like that because this remote event touches on you. You cannot be here without a line of descent that goes back to 1350.

We should not ignore the seepage of caring in some trick of time or numeracy. The trick is also a way of indulging our failure to grasp the facts about the frailty of our vain species. Our history may be coming down to whether we can keep faith with insignificant but unique lives in the great rush of death and the lofty worldliness with which the Trump sighs of glory. Every Vag has a dream of Valhalla.

MISSTEPS IN THE DARK

In considering the epic tremors, I am determined to hold on to small things—a split in the seat of one's pants, a wildflower at Auschwitz, bees gathering at Borodino as the cannon fall silent.

There is an enchanting passage in *War and Peace*, where Tolstoy pauses to think of bees, stinging a child to make it cry, or engaging in the process of pollination to make honey. So what are bees for? Tolstoy cannot answer and he did not know what we know today, that the population of bees has declined by maybe 80 percent, because of parasites or pesticides, because of untender husbandry or the silent sweep of global warming. All the novelist can say is:

"The final purpose of the bee is exhausted neither by the one [explanation], nor the other nor the third purpose that human reason is able to discover. The higher human reason rises in the discovery of these purposes, the more obvious for it is the inaccessibility of the final purpose.

"All that is accessible to man is the observation of the correspondence between the life of a bee and other phenomena of life. It is the same for the purposes of historical figures and peoples."

With all the diaries in the world, and diarists busy recording life, the thing itself—the enterprise and the show—might come to a stop. So let the diarists breathe and have nothing happen to them now and then. It is in those interstices in our smothering literary concrete that flowers of story may spring up.

Or, if you prefer another metaphor, suppose a diarist were recording in fine detail how life went from five past three, to ten past, until hickory dickory dock, the mouse ran up the clock.

I remember a story that when the Mossad went to Argentina to find Adolf Eichmann in 1960, they identified him because he bought flowers on what they knew was his wife's birthday. I may have got the details of this wrong, but I like the speck of odd human interest in the great melodrama—did Adolf curse his sentimentality when he knew he was found out, or did he muster some sour irony about bad luck? So many utilitarians and rationalists cling to the myth of luck.

Or ask yourself whether this is a story, or just a speck in the ongoingness of it all. On *Sunday, April 26th*, in Charlottesville, Virginia, Dr. Lorna Breen killed herself. She was medical director of the New York–Presbyterian Allen Hospital, where she had been working all hours in the struggle to treat people with the coronavirus. "She tried to do her job, and it killed her," said her father, who was also a doctor. Dr. Breen was described as a hero in her work. She was forty-nine. She had herself contracted the virus, and apparently recovered. But she went back to work very soon and was physically and emotionally exhausted in the ordeal. She was a Christian, and a degree of despair is possible. Her family had intervened and taken her from New York to Virginia. Nothing else need be said or known about her life. She may become the subject of a TV movie one day, if such things persist, but it is decent to leave her case open so we may imagine the state of mind of a doctor in that crisis.

Or consider Richard Marek, who died on March 25. He was eighty-six and he had been a notable publisher. He had brought Thomas Harris's *The Silence of the Lambs* and Robert Ludlum's *The Bourne Identity* into print, and he had also been instrumental in the publication of Ernest Hemingway's *A Moveable Feast* . . .

Some time in 1962 or '63, Mr. Marek was riding the New York subway. He was in his late twenties, and eager to get home to read. That day, his boss at the publishing house of Scribner had given him a special assignment. They had just received the pages of what would be *A Moveable Feast*, a memoir of Hemingway's life in Paris in the 1920s.

Hemingway was dead, of course; he had shot himself in July 1961; that signal succumbing of grace to pressure. Marek must have been stirred by that. Thereafter, Papa's widow, Mary, had gathered together the pieces that would be *A Moveable Feast*. It's not clear whether she simply retrieved a file of essays Hemingway had written, or did she (and others?) organize the material and even touch it up? Where had the title come from? Was it Papa's choice or something his friend A. E. Hotchner said he remembered Hemingway talking about? "If you are lucky enough to have lived in Paris as a young man, then wherever you go for the rest of your life, it stays with you, for it is a moveable feast."

Isn't it pretty to think so (words Hemingway did write)? The nostalgic epitaph became central in the cultural placing of Hemingway, just as it nourished the idea of Paris as a lure for tourists. There is a tender touch of advertising in the title.

Never mind that. It's not essential to the story of Richard Marek. This is what had happened to him. In preparation for working at home, Marek had put the Hemingway manuscript pages in a large envelope and taken to the subway.

He must have been thrilled, not just to read Papa's authentic typescript, but by the publishing coup and a significant step in his own career.

Then he left the envelope on the train.

That was the story he told; that was the disaster that had befallen him. Is it hard to swallow? Would it help if, perchance, news of the assassination of John F. Kennedy was passed along the train? If that date doesn't quite fit, was it a report from the West Coast that the Yankees had beaten the Giants one to nothing in the seventh game of the World Series? Or do you prefer an indigent violinist who had stilled the carriage with his sketches from Bach? Had Marek started to read the Henry James paperback in his pocket and become so absorbed, or lost in Kate Croy? Or did Mr. Marek notice a girl sitting opposite him? In a white dress, with a parasol? On the subway? He was married already, but he might have been knocked out for an instant by that passenger. Isn't it easier (or kinder) to believe such possibilities than to think Mr. Marek simply forgot his treasure and his opportunity and left it on the train?

He said he wept all night. I don't think it's stretching the point to have him crying out in his apartment and his world, "This is a disaster!"

At first light (8 a.m., or whenever) the following day he went to the subway lost and found office. He had no great hopes, but he was blessed. *The envelope had been handed in;* nothing had been taken. On the brink of calamity, Marek had been given wings. I believe this happened (more or less), but I know that I have no rational reason for trusting the misstep.

There can be vagaries and intrusions in the most orderly mental constructs. We have to go back no further than 1760 to find this sensible policy:

"Believe me, good folks this is not so inconsiderable a thing as many of you may think it—you have all, I dare say, heard of the animal spirits, as how they are transfused from father to son, &c. &c.—and a great deal to that purpose—Well, you may take my word, that nine parts in ten of a man's sense or his nonsense, his successes and miscarriages in this world depend upon their motions and activity, and the different tracks and trains you put them into, so that when they are once set a-going, whether right or wrong, 'tis not a halfpenny matter.—away they go cluttering like hey-go-mad; and by treading the same steps over and over again, they presently make a road of it, as plain and as smooth as a garden-walk, which, when they are once used to, the Devil himself sometimes shall not be able to drive them off it."

As I said, that is 1760, and the first chapter to volume 1 of *The Life and Opinions of Tristram Shandy, Gentleman*, by Laurence Sterne. Don't you feel that Sterne understands the nature of railways? But George Stephenson, inventor of the Rocket, had not been born yet. Truly, there is something in the theory of brain waves taking us, and throwing us off the rails.

Poor Tristram is about to be the victim of such a misstep. His father and his mother are apparently caught up in the enterprise that may lead to his conception, when the mother is practical or ill-advised enough in his advancing passion to ask, "Pray my dear, have you not forgot to wind up the clock?" Is there a mouse in the clock yet?

This wayward question is too much for the father's equilibrium winding up his delivery system. "Good G-!" he cried. "Did ever woman, since the creation of the world, interrupt a man with such a silly question?"

All of which leads Tristram to wonder how the homunculus that would be a part of him had been jostled, vexed, disarrayed, and discombobulated by his mother's remark. As if the clock needed winding more thoroughly than her husband's good intentions and the process of conception. As if a pilgrim of literature could leave a precious text on the S train.

Are there brain waves in locomotion? Are we helpless in our addiction to similarities? I was reminded . . .

in a valise

In 1920–21, in Chicago, where he was writing freelance for the *Toronto Star Weekly*, and working on his first short stories, Hemingway met Hadley Richardson. He was twenty-one and she was twenty-nine. They fell in love, and Hemingway would later speak with reverence of his feeling, as if she was the great love of his life. Though he kept an open mind. They were married in September 1921 and soon they went to live in Paris. They would have a son, Jack or "Bumby," in 1923, and Hemingway wrote with pathos about the hard, true, simple life they led in Paris. In fact, they managed on money Hadley had inherited, enough to make their Parisian life better than simple in what was a good time for the dollar.

Still, Hemingway was often away on journalistic trips, and Hadley seemed to be upset at being left. He was a very handsome man, daring or reckless, with a romantic sense of himself. In 1925, the couple met Pauline Pfeiffer, who would be Hemingway's second wife one day. I mention these things simply to raise the possibility that missteps have origins and reasons.

In 1922, Hemingway went to Lausanne to cover one of the peace conferences that Europe was sporting in those days. The stars at this eleven-week get-together were Lord Curzon, İsmet İnönü, and Mussolini. Hemingway urged Hadley to join him there to overcome their quarrels over prior separations. She agreed to make the trip. As she prepared to go to the Gare de Lyon, she took Hemingway's work in progress—several short stories—and packed them in a valise, so he could develop them. She even included the carbon copies.

This may have seemed more than thoughtful. She took a taxi to the station and a porter helped her load the luggage. Then she thought to get some water for the journey, and when she returned with it moments later—the valise that held the manuscripts was gone. It has never been found.

Hemingway would say he "had never seen anyone hurt by a thing other than death or unbearable suffering, except Hadley when she told me about the things being gone." She wept and cried, before she had revealed the nature of the loss. He reassured her that nothing could be that bad and then she spelled it out. "I was sure that she could not have brought the carbons, too," he said. He got someone to cover for him in Lausanne and rushed back to Paris to scour their apartment. But the carbons were not there, and the author admitted he did something bad that night. It may have involved a prostitute. It was a thing he didn't want to talk about, though he had raised it in the first place.

I have tried to fill this chapter with an unedited but suggestive medley of incidents, going from the fatal action of Dr. Lorna Breen to the comedy of the Shandy family. This may seem haphazard or digressive—Sterne thought digression was the sunshine of reading; others have wondered whether digression is really possible in a format where readers read one word after another and try to accommodate a sentence.

It is not clear what followed on the loss of the valise at the Gare de Lyon—if only Sherlock Holmes had still been around. Did Hemingway know some of his stories by heart? Did he recompose them, possibly to their benefit? Or were some stories lost forever? Ernest and Hadley carried on for a few years. They traveled, they skied; they went to bullfights; they had their son. Hemingway's fortunes improved and they knew a lot of the right people. It's evident that Hadley was devastated by the loss, that she saw it as a disaster. Was that having to admit her neglect, or having to digest the rage her husband expressed? What did he cry out? Decades later, telling the story, Hadley still seemed in pain. Was that because the incident, the loss or her carelessness, had grown out of distress at how the marriage was faring? It's very hard to separate the fictional potential in what happened from the plain, inexplicable facts. Neither of the couple seemed ever to have forgotten the incident.

Ernest had three more wives after Hadley. She had a second marriage, to Paul Mowrer, a journalist she had met in Paris in the late '20s. Hadley died only in 1979, at the age of eighty-seven. So she could have read *A Moveable Feast* as well as *Across the River and into the Trees* (1950), in which the author, a wounded soldier, imagines a young lover. In history, the corpses all lie dreaming.

◆

In the comfortable bourgeois way of things, we like to have our disasters no more perilous than the breakup of a marriage, the early death of a parent, or the difficulty of finding good Sage Derby cheese. This scale of mishap or disadvantage is meant to be commonplace, and finally comic if measured against the scale of the Black Death or the Indian tsunami of 2004. But a broken marriage is no joke, and maybe its undermining of an institution was more damaging in the twentieth century than all the impact of wars. Love is one of the most vibrant hopes humans entertain, and to see it spoiled may be a common source of anxiety or depression. But the idea of "falling in love" is so romantic, or religious. The falling tends to take an upwards incline, even if we sometimes overlook the blunt fact of lovers falling down—to the ground, to the floor, to something like a bed—to be meshed in sex, the drive that propels so many of us into schematics of love.

It is a helpless part of humanist aspiration that we want to interpret ourselves, and it is the uncertain orthodoxy that we say, look, here is a great love . . . or can't you see, this is a disaster. When biology, survival, the theory of the fittest, was surging ahead like a blind shark. So Tristram may or may not have been unsettled by his mother's ill-timed question and his father's snorting disbelief. The code of lost manuscripts in the overall career of Hemingway could be a clue to the principle of nothing mattering like written texts. And Dr. Lorna Breen is a tragedy to be enshrined, or the impulse of an unhappy person who could no longer endure the terrible conflict of learned medicine and rampant microbiological destiny. We want to live but we cannot survive. You are the descendant of the Black Death, still bright with hope so the scars are generally invisible.

The narrative structure of Steven Soderbergh's movie *Contagion* is quite cunning in that Gwyneth Paltrow's character (Beth) is depicted as not just a crucial carrier of the film's virus (MEV-1)—a good deal more lethal than Covid-19.

In addition, Beth is a faithless wife borne along on what is either selfishness or self who has betrayed good old Matt Damon (Mitch) in his view of a happy family existence in Minneapolis with their two children. Sexual attraction is another infection, risky sometimes, but one in which we are prepared to take a risk. But any gesture towards moral condemnation of Gwyneth is futile and beside the point. The virus is faithful to or ready for any available organism. It will fuck anyone. It is a matter of blind chance that Gwyneth shook hands with a food server in Macau who happened to have touched the dread bat contagion. And touch is still measured as a mark of affection and social willingness. Beth seems touchy-feely. That is what we do in the hope of being together. But in *Contagion* the liberated virus takes out 26 million lives worldwide in a few months.

It is a bad thing, but entirely natural. Twenty-six million? So few?

ACROSS THE STREET

Across the street, for a few days now, there has been an orange tent. It has a sporty design; you might expect to see it on a beach in Malibu or on the slopes of Everest. It is a shelter in place, where one—or is it two?—are living, waiting for the distress or disquiet of the "neighborhood" to bring in the uneasy police who have always kept this zip code tidy. But the latest city regulations hedge around the old principle of moving vagrants on. There is a new attempt at kindness, a wish for reform. The mayor has thought of using vacant hotel rooms (tourism is way down) to accommodate the indigent—but the details are proving difficult. There is also apprehension among the police of getting too close to these homeless people, and laying hands on them. But vagrants are obliged to wear a mask now. Failing in that respect could provide leverage.

At the *end of April and the first days of May*, there are so many uncertainties. Our president—who responds to matters of fact as if he had indigestion—does what he calls a town hall meeting for Fox. He does it sitting beneath the Lincoln Memorial. It's not that the message in this placement is obscure; any faith in messaging is evaporating before our eyes. But, *on Sunday, May 3*, with the gravitas of repressed belches, he concedes the need for realism in forecasting casualty figures. Two weeks ago, he had been prepared to reckon on 60,000 dead, with the nonchalance of a seasoned general in a valley of death. But now, at 66,000, he can see there might be 100,000. Every one of them terrible, he says—he has that line pat now, a glib parenthetical—but so much less than bigger bogey numbers. Like 2 million, that black coal tip hanging over us.

Meanwhile, informed reporting suggests places where deaths may be underreported, or counted as not due to the coronavirus. One hundred thousand might turn out modest, but he is self-effacing and demure when it comes to bad news. So *on May 4*, he leaves it to others to admit that the daily death toll from the virus might be 3,000 by June 1. In other words, a lot higher than April knew when April was supposed to be the cruellest month.

The gaps are appearing everywhere, as in those moments in earthquake movies where tentative fissures start to invade the concrete universe. The most informed opinions—from the people who are striving to achieve it—are that it is unlikely that a vaccine can be identified and produced in sufficient quantities before the spring of 2021. There are even warnings that a vaccine might never be found. But beneath the statue of Lincoln,

President Trump opines, "I think we're going to have a vaccine by the end of the year. The doctors would say, Well you shouldn't say that. I'll say what I think. . . . I think we'll have a vaccine sooner than later." And he was right!

There he is, the sturdy voice of American distaste for expertise or science. He could be Jimmy Stewart in the face of intelligent data, just sticking with a hunch that the unlikely American *it* could be done, and looking at the horizon with that dry boyish smile that goes with his drawl. Isn't this a can-do country? Isn't that how the facts of slavery, Native American suppression, and the remorseless exploitation of the land were accomplished with an airy clear conscience and a reassuring smile?

Trump doesn't smile lately. But his downcast comes less from deaths in his land than because his heroic mirror is being dimmed. His face is settling into the jowls of depression, with sometimes a hint of dissociation or entropy. His mind seems to wander, as if dreaming of escape. He is on another plane, not quite mortal perhaps. Only the week before he told a press conference that he wouldn't tell us why he knew that UFO photos were important, as if he had access to some classified intelligence, or as if he felt he was in a story. Like President Reagan, believing he had been there in war because he recalled narrating documentaries about such things.

But Trump sits there beneath the nineteen-foot, white marble Lincoln by Daniel Chester French. Donald is not overawed; he manages to be wistful, philosophical, and finally defiant, like John Wayne's Ethan Edwards (a monumental Vag) confronting the burned mesas of *The Searchers*. This is a West where stupidity is turned into legend as we watch.

This blatant crack where defiance and science are like tectonic plates is borne out in our largest discord. During the month of April, the Trump administration has felt the need to "open up the country" as if it was a form of sexual desire. The government and the Coronavirus Task Force has laid down necessary guidelines for opening up: fourteen days of declining infection; the availability of widespread testing and the tracking of infectious cases; the confidence that hospitals are in a position to treat patients properly.

With varying degrees of tact and worry, Drs. Deborah Birx and Anthony Fauci have tried to explain that the opening up of businesses and the erasure of social distancing, the misguided thought that the virus has been spanked and handled (the success story), could be a prelude to fresh outbreaks, especially in areas of the country that seemed to have been spared—except for those hot spots in meatpacking factories, in prisons, and in nursing homes. Rachel Maddow has been at pains to point out those terrible stories. But the president has ignored nursing homes, disdained prisons, and acted on the conviction that the new America needs meat.

The current record of social distancing is hardly open to debate. California and especially in the Bay Area, where decisions on staying at home in isolation were taken early (although they might have come earlier if Washington had taken a lead), have had striking results.

With a state population of 39.5 million, California has had 54,877 infections and 2,213 deaths. In New York State, with 19.5 million people, there have been nearly 319,000 infections and 25,000 deaths. In the Bay Area (population 7.7 million), there have been 8,593 infections and 309 deaths.

What further lessons do we need to keep that strictness in place, not just to flatten the curve of infections and to have a scheme for testing, but to tame the illness? That project seems to require stringent care throughout the summer. But summer is the business season for so many of us. Even in April, big young crowds appeared on southern Californian beaches, stir-crazy, restless, and "independent." It is also clear that thousands of restaurants will close forever. It is becoming apparent that many schools and colleges would suffer the same fate, as the experience of education became simplified by systems like Zoom. In some eyes, the entire future of sport was in the balance.

But the contest or the debate is far larger. And it turns on an irony so far-reaching that it is generally being ignored. On April 8, Senator Bernie Sanders withdrew from the presidential race for 2020. Not long thereafter, he said that he would support Joe Biden in the contest set for November. At his age—Sanders was seventy-eight—it was unlikely that he would be able to mount another presidential race.

Yet, that same April, the president Sanders had meant to oppose was putting into practice the largest redistribution of capital that the country had ever witnessed. Donald Trump didn't think of this as socialism. He acted as if in an emergency. He was coughing up $2 trillion straightaway, just as some economists thought it could soon be $6 trillion or $10 trillion. Inevitably, and under the stress of the health crisis, the new America would be bound to adopt universal health care. Nor did one have to be discerning to foresee drastic alterations in the country's treatment of property, housing, education, race, immigration—and the concept of employment. All of a sudden, and under a helpless Republican administration, America was having a revolution. How soon would Republicans notice this and feel duped? Or on the brink of disaster?

Before reaching that lofty condition, the United States would have so many other things to negotiate. Experienced medical researchers (like Dr. Fauci) and authoritative commentators (like Donald G. McNeil) were predicting a natural epidemiological response to the opening up gestures for the economy. By the late summer and early fall there would be fresh spikes of infection, and new spurts of death. Those words, "spikes" and "spurts," seem nasty but manageable—all the more so if testing and tracking were really in effect.

You see, I do not want to anthropomorphize the virus. It has no willful design, no dramatic character. It is simply growth for growth's sake, the way an embryo may be growing in the womb. Spurts and spikes do give a hint of some Sugar Ray jabbing at an opponent. Whereas the virus is as impersonal and undirected as a tide coming in.

But spurts and spikes are loaded with threat and energy. Without our antisocial measures, the distancing and the absence of touch or shared air, our brief, chill calm could go haywire in the summer. Then the curve might rise again like Moby Dick eager to rebuke and drown the vanity of Ahab. The coronavirus might have its fullest career in the winter of 2020–21. Then grasp two other possibilities: the failure to get a vaccine; and the chance that the virus might mutate. As yet, in 2020, it had had a modest death rate. For many victims there were few symptoms, and the likelihood of recovery. But suppose the sting of the virus became stronger and more fatal. Suppose it gained the potency of the Black Death, or the 1665 plague that Daniel Defoe had described in his *Journal*.

It is possible that that wave of illness killed close to a quarter of the people living in London. King Charles II removed his court to the sweeter air of Oxford to have a better perspective on the plague. There were leading medical people (they might even call themselves scientists) ready to analyze the data and make predictions about what it was and where it was going. It was apparent even then that the illness was most deadly in the congested areas around the City, a network of overcrowded streets and alleys, and with few of the best amenities to counter poverty.

Defoe described this as a clear-eyed journalist and a man who believed in survival and the ingenuity of mankind caught in a crisis. In *Robinson Crusoe* (1719) he had made ordeal romantic in its view of Crusoe coming through. He is shipwrecked—on a vessel in the slave trade. There is something rapturous in the passage where Crusoe returns to his lost ship and avails himself of so many valuable provisions, weapons, and comforts, before it sinks. It is there that *Crusoe* becomes a glorious celebration of the camping instinct and of man taming the wilderness.

It was three years later that Defoe published his *Journal of the Plague Year*—he had been five when the plague struck London, living close to its center—and it is a book that anyone close to disaster needs to keep in his or her pocket. It was less the child's recollection than a tough-minded adult estimate of human nature, but in his *Journal* Defoe says that there had been the hope that the populace would have learned a lot from the test. He had hoped to see "a new face, so the manners of the people had a new appearance . . . but it must be acknowledged that the general practice of the people was just as it was before, and very little difference was to be seen. Some, indeed, said things were worse; that the morals of the people, hardened by the danger they had been in, like seamen after a storm is over, were more wicked and more stupid, more bold and hardened, in their vices and immoralities than they were before."

Sometimes one can think that people are the great disaster, and innocence the essential affectation.

◆

On May 4 still, a sunny morning, city officials came to remove the orange tent. It was parked next to the curb, like a vehicle. The workers wore white protective clothes and their compacting truck scooped up the tent and a mattress inside it like bodies.

(We have to realize that the whole matter of corpse disposal is quite vexing, just as funerals can no longer be public events.)

The occupants of the tent had gone away. Our son, Zachary, met them on the street last night, two young men, one black, one white. He says they did not speak well, as if they might be mentally ill. One talked of Dungeons and Dragons and said he was new to the city and looking for friends. He wondered if he could come inside our house, but Zachary said no chance.

Old lady: I believe you have a wise son.

Author: We are grateful for him every day.

Old lady: So that unfortunate affair on your street got tidied up.

Author: Madam, we are nowhere near a tidy success story. This situation is not going to get any better.

Old lady: Well not in my time, let's hasten to add. But I have had great days, I assure you, even if I now seem an old woman. May I share an amusing remark with you?

Author: It would be most welcome.

Old lady: That Dr. Birx—if she knotted together all her scarves and shawls, she might be able to escape from the prison.

Author: A Rapunzel?

THE NUMBERS

Had it been the old May, there would be cricket being played on English fields. Last weekend would have seen the 146th running of the Kentucky Derby. There would be marches and parties for Cinco de Mayo. But *this May 5*, we are shut away watching the ghost of such things through the silence of thick windows.

Not everything is still. Today, at the new height of our anxiety, with intimations that 134,000 might be dead by August 1, there is news on the *Guardian* website of an old acquaintance, or someone we have known, and who has been overlooked in this crisis. The website has a high-angle photograph of parched ground cracking up in the heat, with a single figure walking in the top left-hand part of the frame. Under the rubric of "Climate change," there is the headline, "One billion people will live in insufferable heat within fifty years."

A paper has been published in the *Proceedings of the National*

Academy of Science and it forecasts that some areas of Earth are overheating, taking their inhabitants beyond the "comfortable niche" of temperatures in the range from 43 degrees Fahrenheit to 82. Maybe 30 percent of the world's population would be compelled to live in what we now call Saharan conditions. One of the authors of the paper, Professor Marten Scheffer from Wageningen University, in the Netherlands, said, "I think it is fair to say that average temperatures over 29 Centigrade [84 Fahrenheit] are unlivable. You'd have to move or adapt. But there are limits to adaptation. If you have enough money and energy, you can use air conditioning and fly in food and then you might be OK. But that is not the case for most people."

Just in an attempt at empathy, or seeking the other fellow's predicament, I can understand that there are problems in flying stuff in our new qualified life. Yes, I can imagine aircraft carrying food. They might start out as official transportation. Air Force One, if you like, but then in some short space of time that might be downgraded to private maverick aircraft, or an Air Force One with the president having to fly the damn plane himself in the scattered herd of rich guys in their nonchalant cockpits. We have seen these movies, like the Rock in his red chopper.

So this magical freighted aircraft—with Scotch salmon on ice; raspberries picked in Somerset in June perfection; and Brazilian coffee beans, plus twelve cartons of toilet paper, and why not a Stormy or two to comb the master's hair?—needs somewhere safe to land. Well, that can be arranged, can't it? Though you will have noted that major airlines, the carriers, are already fidgeting over new business plans. Their fleets of aircraft are lined up at airports, like the mosaic tiles of new automobiles that will not be sold. How long before those runways crumble at the edges and wildflowers pierce the tarmac? How long before planes have not been serviced lately enough to be reliable?

In which case, it is possible that the culture of the private plane and the secret airstrip gains hold. These things will need careful guarding and secure stocks of jet fuel. Not so long ago, flying was a harebrained, seat-of-the-pants operation. Wild flyboys with the right stuff crashed in planes made of matchwood. We could be getting back to something like that. Or, to put it another way, you may have had your last travail with airport security, slipping off your shoes and being X-rayed. If you have the money and a gun, you may be able to fly as you like. You may have to learn to fly yourself in the end. Be like Harrison Ford, a geriatric Han Solo. Or Doris Day in *Julie* (1956), where she plays a former flight attendant who has to land an airliner. Didn't you always hope to be Doris Day?

Oh, Lord, you say, even if you're laughing. This is so unfair. For won't we handle this unforeseen crisis and scoff at a future catastrophe that is still in doubt or an academic argument? This old Earth of ours may not get so savagely warm, and we can get back to normal, just as Jared Kushner has promised.

Six months ago, we had not dreamed of the coronavirus. Only a few people like Bill Gates had surmised that something like it was the greatest danger we faced—though at the level of "we," Gates had a few advantages. Six months ago, it was my naïve reckoning that the proper climax to this book would be to look at the prospects for climate "difficulty" and the dilemmas that presented. I would remind readers of the Paris Climate Accords (they rather insisted on those capital letters, instead of settling on lowercase and humility) of 2015. That United Nations conference of 196 nations had agreed to ask for a limit to global warming of no more than 2 degrees Celsius compared with pre-industrial temperatures.

That was five years ago, and in the time since then there have been shortfalls in national efforts and commitment to the recommendations. Donald Trump has ordered the United States out of the accords and the very uncertain measures that had been meant to enforce them. There had never been a hint of compulsion or inescapable instruction. But even those who were pledged to the accords may forget the widespread warning by experts in 2015 that the brave new limits were inadequate. As well as unenforceable, without some dictatorial power with total firepower and compelled obedience, something we were rather against. It is not cynicism, but common sense, to conclude from the Paris exercise that climate was out of our control, so that unmitigated weather was coming down our road. The most irresistible conclusion was that with this infinite disaster portending, it was up to human beings to make the best of it, to secure the aircraft, the guns, and the toilet paper, and have the fucking best time while they could.

Old lady: Sir! You go too far! I do not like that word in a proper book. Not when the sense of it is so upsetting.

Author: I apologize. I will reconsider the word in proof—

Old lady: Hah! You're thinking I won't be here by then. But I should assure you, I am not that kind of prim "old lady." If that word troubles me, it may be just because it does not quite apply to me anymore.

Author: I know that feeling.

Old lady: It happens. Didn't we sit together to watch a Kentucky Derby once?

Author: We did. It was the last one you ever saw.

Old lady: Sir, you're playing fast and loose with me, having me dead and alive.

Author: That is writing, I believe.

Old lady: You understand, my true upset was at thinking this sweet world was being baked past freshness. Must you be so blunt and gloomy about that?

Author: Not so long ago, but before our virus, I was having dinner with my publisher. I outlined this theory of those who are past caring. And he told me I had to say that in the book.

Old lady: So he cares. You bastard.

Author: Don't flirt with me.

◆

I hope no one reading this book is in any doubt over my regard for Donald Trump. He is the worst personal disaster this country has ever faced. That is bad enough, but we elected him president. He is despicable yet stupid, dangerous and incompetent, pathologically dishonest and consistently devious. You can point to particular failings: the refusal to engage in scientific or evidentiary thinking (because that would imply some reference to authority outside himself); giving up on the Paris Climate Accords; the racial bigotry; the scheme of corruption so quotidian that it is no longer noticed; the lack of family life; the appalling vulgarity; the inability to do up his jacket.

All of that was on full display before he had been lazily indifferent about his own intelligence warnings on the virus. To be followed by an inability to organize a response that could mitigate the tragedy, and then a frenzied awareness that since blame and guilt were in the air, everyone else must line up for the custard pie. In the squalor of his inner room there was a moment when he identified the disaster, and was desperate to devour its opportunity.

Not that he was insightful or even articulate about it—he has abandoned grammar or sense in so many appearances. He prefers improv to any written and recited speech. He regards that as liberty. He feels his energy is being restricted by text, and his puffed-up face with its pinched-anus mouth testify to his dread of repression. He is the actor who knows he must transcend what the playwright wrote. This is another assertion of narcissism, that he does not mean to be communicative so much as "on," and that is enough. So he grunted and sighed when he said the country had to open up. There were clouds of self-pity in his head. But he indicated the America he wanted to make great again when he said that without open businesses, there wouldn't be a country.

But I think he was correct, and that is the most damning point in the whole story.

Out of threatened instinct, he sensed the nullity of his America once deprived of merciless competition. And in the shadow of disaster he began to intuit the cruel light of throwing off all old rules and sentiments. He had tried on the persona of General in a War, and that had failed because he was too undisciplined for service. So perhaps he would be the monster master of the universe, capricious, vicious, and entertaining. Wasn't that his history and a tradition we had been picking up?

The simple act of congregation, of meeting strangers, was in doubt. In person, as opposed to versions of impersonality. For a while, staying at home was greeted with awe. Not every family was simply delighted by the opportunity of being together: there was a higher incidence of domestic abuse; and under the guise of being "stir-crazy" we were feeling imprisoned. The opening up being offered as an alternative was elemental, psychological, and spiritually above and beyond going to church or hiking the Pacific trail. More than most, America was a country founded in mobility, the desperate getting away from one thing and into another, even if that other was only the decor of imagination.

The cessation of transport, and the death of oil, constituted just one aspect of the way the economy had taken on symptoms of malaise that went from ruinous to fatal with a speed noticed in corona. There was shopping only for food and medicine, and so we recognized shopping was an exercise as profound as sex. An array of occupations were cut dead in their tracks. In a few weeks

30 million people were unemployed. It was pedantry to say this was a recession and not a depression, and willful escapism to miss the suddenness of its arrival. If there was upheaval in six weeks, what of the next six days? We had thought vaguely that the end of the world was due towards the end of the twenty-first century. Had we been misled? As if hooked on the ads?

We were into an era of astounding contradictions that went unobserved by authority so that a new calm instability prevailed. Thus there were longer lines at food banks and warnings about Americans starving while surplus milk was being poured away into dry prairies, and vegetables were ploughed back into the ground. Then the vaunted Coronavirus Task Force was reconsidered. This had had press conferences every day in which Trump rambled through monologues without an interior. But against the assigned script, the virus was as jumpy as the Alien monster in a Midwest drawing room.

So the task force was sent to rewrite: it might become "advisory"—as if this man understood the theory of advice. Death rates were climbing in hitherto unknown places with emphasis on rural states that were starting to fall in line with "hot spots." Some places have gorges and rivers; some have prisons and meat plants. It was harder and harder to believe that the American president cared about the deaths, or had feeling for relatives of the corpses. Did he even notice them, or was he giving up on press conferences as a way of being separated from the dead? In the short, frenzied history of the pandemic, he had not once visited a hospital or a place where health workers were putting themselves at grave risk to save or treat his people.

Had those people, we plaintive idiots, been bought off at $1,200 a head? Was that the blunt deal of our slavery? Was that enough to erase bad dreams of where we were headed: into a winter of vanished jobs, and depleted income; into a time of crushed property values and chronic anxiety. In addition, we were beginning to see the possible future of "education," that leading people out of darkness. The school year of 2019–20 had had to be curtailed. Students were sent home. Some rearrangement of fee payments had to be worked out. And the designated parties tried to develop online forms of teaching that would suffice in the underlying transaction: the payment of a sum of money (seldom small) for a degree.

What was the lesson for education? Maybe those hallowed sites of learning, the Ivy League, would become derelict properties. The wisdom and experience of teachers could be reassessed as "input." And the provision of degrees for payment endured without pretentious fuss over pass/fail evaluations. But that cast the recent history of education in a very bad light even if it had been an ongoing travesty to say that college degrees and high school diplomas reflected profound awareness or the ability to treat evidence.

The disaster in education had been building for decades. The advertising for an informed, modern nation was screwed. About 3.7 million kids were graduating high school, while approximately

2 million bachelor's degrees were awarded in a year. But only 12 percent of Americans are reckoned to read and write at a high school graduate level. The country seemed to know less of its own history; it was increasingly inarticulate; it could find no way to ameliorate the difficulties of race or the burden of poverty; it was at a loss over how to deal with climate change. Could it see that the coronavirus was only a rehearsal for a bigger ordeal?

That was the tip of the iceberg for revisionist thinking and any chance of a reformed America. The virus was only an illness and it was becoming clear that the man in charge—how could this singularity be so in a contract that spoke of "we the people"?— was prepared to accommodate so many more casualties than medicine could contemplate. If there had to be a few million, or as many as it would take, so be it, just be sure that there is a system for disposing of the bodies and their tents swiftly, because corpses can be embarrassing.

Corona had been an open-sesame; it had made manifest the wretched state of poverty in America. The NPR show *Marketplace* did a survey early in May. This was from a program that was usually jaunty about "doing the numbers" and making us float on the ascent of the Dow. The show was an ad like so many others, masquerading as news reportage. But its survey asked the question: how many Americans would have trouble paying an unexpected bill for $250. Salmon, raspberries, toilet paper, and a cut-price Stormy and we're way past $250. But the survey found that 40 percent of Americans would have that trouble, and the number was 59 percent if it concentrated on black Americans.

Or on the road?

    The greatness that Donald Trump was so desperate to return to, the power of numbers and a liberated Dow—gangbusters, he would say—was like a hologram, or an assertion that tried to obliterate the actual circumstances of monthly or daily close calls, of people being constitutionally hard up. Or of the poverty that was only a week away from having a tent (it is best not to have it orange, that color might draw attention) as a home on the street.

    Or on the road?

OUR ROAD

"When he woke in the woods in the dark and the cold of the night he'd reach out to touch the child sleeping beside him."

So touch is still allowed in Cormac McCarthy's *The Road*— that may be the only advantage it has over our predicament in the early summer of 2020. They say it is going to be warm and pleasant in the West. "They" keep saying such things, as if they were programmed long ago. "Have a nice day" becomes a macabre salute.

There was a woman once, mother to the boy and wife to the man. But the situation and its likelihood were too forbidding for her and so she killed herself—that seemed reasonable and its common sense hangs in the boy's mind like Christmas or demons.

This is the point to say that in the motion picture of *The Road*, the mother gets her flashback scene where she is Charlize Theron. (The actress had played a part in setting up the movie, recommending the novel to a producer.) Now, strictly in cinematic terms, Theron may be anathema to suicide or walking away into the woods forever. But the woman saw that the man had used one of their only three pistol bullets to kill a marauder. So they were short a death, the escape, and that's why she removed herself. Theron may seem gratuitous in the movie, but that doesn't protect McCarthy from suspicion that he didn't know how to write a woman in this ordeal.

Something has happened before *The Road*, but we do not know what it was. In descriptions of the book this is said to be an "extinction event." But there are some people left, a few, and none of them can be trusted. On the back of my Vintage paperback it says that the book is set in America, but that is not admitted in the text. Of course, Cormac McCarthy is American (born in Rhode Island, living often in Tennessee, and now hidden away in New Mexico), and when I read the novel I imagined a setting like eastern Oregon. But that is because I am attracted to that semidesert place and feel it has been neglected. All the book says is that the man and the boy are walking across desolate country, going south in some expectation of reaching the coast. This could be Oregon on the way to a shoreline north of San Francisco. I am thinking of wild country where civilization has never proved itself. Parts of the movie were shot in northwestern Pennsylvania, Louisiana, and Oregon, but it could have been Siberia, the winter plateau of Spain, or anywhere. We feel that whatever has happened has affected all the world.

But neither McCarthy nor the man cares to say what this disaster was. So in our open mind we have to consider nuclear on-slaught, a plague, or economic cataclysm. And we are open to other possibilities, some radical intervention. It's not quite the nuclear blowup, because there is no sense of toxic fallout; no symptoms of plague are mentioned; and there is no legend of all the Wall Streets collapsing. The single sign of catastrophe is the quantity of ash that seems ubiquitous. That does remind me of the popular legend that after the asteroid struck the area of the Yucatan so long ago (do you remember? sixty-six million years earlier), there was darkness in the air and then a smothering de-posit of something like ash.

What happened before *The Road* is less important than the nothing that can be done about it. Or not for several million years—and you do have some conception of the patience that will require, as well as an understanding that it may have been impatience that prompted the "extinction event," or boredom. The man and the boy do not think of saving the world—that im-modesty is pointless. They are attempting to survive, or endure, one day after the other. Though the boy is beset with eroding thoughts that not to survive could be gentler and even more natural now. After all, humans do not survive.

There are gas stations along the way, dry and forsaken. There are townships and even cities in the same deserted condition. But that physical devastation is in the overcast of there being no cen-tral authority or organization. Government is gone. There is no news because there is no broadcasting, no newspapers, no Inter-net. There is no way in which any gesture towards leadership can speak to the people. There are no cell phones, no trumpets, no need to witness a whining bully leader, and his rhetoric about opening up. This world is so open it's naked, desolate and bereft. There were disaster fables once—like *San Andreas*—buoyed by a terrific, inane program of rebuilding. But ruin is now the ubiquitous constant, like winter, and it has become so cold now.

"With the first gray light he rose and left the boy sleeping and walked out to the road and squatted and studied the country to the south. Barren, silent, godless. He thought the month was October but he wasn't sure. He hadn't kept a calendar for years. They were moving south. There'd be no surviving another winter here."

"The road" does seem to refer to a real road, but there is no sense of it as a numbered highway that goes anywhere. The possibility of maps is in doubt, though the man does have a torn guide to the land that he tries to fathom. He and the boy have a makeshift cart for their few things—a tarpaulin against the rain (they do not have a tent), a few food things and the water they have stolen or found—sometimes in shattered buildings there is spilled grain, or even shelves of canned vegetables. But the age of plunder is past; so little is left now. They have the pistol, too, but no books, no souvenirs or photo albums, no mineshafts into their roots or history. They are not clinging to a treasured small Vuillard painting or a recording of the last Ravel string quartets.

There are some others on the road—loners or even gangs that may have vehicles and the bleak plan for making slaves of anyone they find, of raping them, or keeping them for a cannibal dinner. There is a time at which these two come upon an underground room packed with these slaves who have no future except that of being eaten. It is the point in *The Road* where McCarthy comes closest to a conventional horror story or our nightmares of what the concentration camps were like. That nostalgia.

So the road is not quite a given or reliable connection; it is the last stage of wilderness that has given up the thought of being attached to human purpose. As the man and the boy move on it, the road is losing destination. It is turning into a lifeline—so faint or indiscernible among other trails in the forest. As hard as he strives, for the boy and himself, the man is ill. We do not know his condition; there are no doctors to define it, to be hopeful or advise caution. Diagnosis and treatment have been erased by anxiety. The man may be scarred by toxicity in the ash, by malnutrition and exposure. He may have a preexisting condition, also known as life, and he is on a timer.

"There were fires still burning high in the mountains and at night they could see the light from them deep orange in the snowfall. It was getting colder but they had campfires all night and left them burning behind them when they set out again in the morning. He'd wrapped their feet in sacking tied with cord and so far the snow was only a few inches deep but he knew that if it got much deeper they would have to leave the cart. Already it was hard going and he stopped often to rest. Slogging to the edge of the road with his back to the child where he stood bent with his hands on his knees, coughing. He raised up and stood with weeping eyes. On the gray snow a fine mist of blood."

Their being together, father and son, is the most frightening thing of all. Of course, they are companions as well as being linked by blood or family line. So they speak together and they hunch over the campfire called taking care of each other. But they are waiting for one of them to perish—there is no escaping that game of risk—and they contemplate the being left alone like anyone mindful of a plague close at hand. So the bullets are as precious as they are fatal. The father has taught the boy how to shoot himself. He wonders if he might have to execute his beloved if the predatory stink of some living dead comes after them.

Nearly all *The Road* is set out of doors—if only because so few doors are left, with every remaining structure poised between being a shelter or a trap. It is no longer so great a stretch of the imagination to wonder whether our homes might be close to that ambiguity. For homelessness could become a universal state, the abode of the masses. When the virus hits the southern hemisphere there are going to be millions under pressure of starvation and they are going to move northwards to survive. In our proudest, niftiest cities the mile-long lines at food banks (they exist already) may turn their hungry attention to those despised streets of plenty, the neighborhoods where readers live. How many degrees of separation from the gourmet to the cannibal?

Oh no, you say, looking for an old lady to assist you. That could never happen, not in this world we have made. But just consider how recently you were blind and deaf and unknowing about this now of ours. *On February 19, 2020,* I went to New York for the memorial tribute to Sonny Mehta, my publisher and friend. There were about five hundred of us in the Celeste Bartos Auditorium at the New York Public Library, book people. There were fine speakers, and we were in no doubt about being at the end of a great era. Publishing would never be the same. How little we guessed then what it soon might be. Disaster can come as quick as a tiger.

In the wild, McCarthy is bound to describe what we once regarded as nature. He talks of the sky, the light, the hills, the forest. There is so much on ash and the bracken that they scavenge for firewood. But the novel is oppressively without the uplift of nature or the glow and the growing. The natural world is in entropy. There seem to be no animals or birds, and fish are gone from the streams. Is that part of the extinction, or is it a measure of the nihilism that the river feels?

This nullity in the external world looms over the bond between the man and the boy. They are father and son, and the father understands that a child will have panic fears of what may be coming down the road to get them. The child has no name, but he speaks to his Papa. The father rallies the boy's spirits and tells him stories. But the boy is not a fool or a dreamer. He knows the tenuousness of being alive, and the dread, and he is close to a despond or fatigue because of it. Without religion, they are pilgrims. They pass through a ghost city and see "a corpse in a doorway dried to leather." They discuss the bad things in their heads and the father tells him: "You forget what you want to remember and you remember what you want to forget."

It's a chilling line and some of us may find it gets at the curious missteps in your thought process developing in these days of corona. That could frighten you off trying to read this grim but burnished book. I am not going to recommend it, not if P. G. Wodehouse is a possible alternative. But I am traditionalist enough not to "spoil" it for you by giving away the ending. The resolution of the plot is a touch abrupt and not good, yet not as rough as you feared. But the very final paragraph is tender for an earlier nature or the moment when a sense of the Earth was still precious and colored by the light:

"Once there were brook trout in the streams in the mountains. You could see them standing in the amber current where the white edges of their fins dimpled softly in the flow. They smelled of moss on your hand. Polished and muscular and torsional. On their backs were vermiculate patterns that were maps of the world in its becoming. Maps and mazes. Of a thing which could not be put back. Not be made right again. In the deep glens where they lived all things were older than man and they hummed of mystery."

I want to say that this is a great book, and one that you should read. But that is a tough call. As I reread the book in advance of doing this chapter, I was often sick to my stomach with dread or terror about how one talks to children in a time of plague or alleged extinction. Just as I would not recommend anyone about taking up a career as an actor or a writer—it has to be their solitary responsibility—so I am hesitant with *The Road*.

◆

The novel was published in 2006, and it is no more than 70,000 words, without chapters or substantial breaks. It comes as an unrelenting but impassive stream of prose, and I doubt I'm alone in having read it or inhaled it in a day. Not that it makes breathing relaxed; not that the book pretends to be less than a challenge to complacency and an ordinary desire to feel good.

The novel is dedicated to McCarthy's son, John Francis, born when the author was in his sixties; the boy was eight as the novel was published, and that seems about the age of the character. The tenderness of the relationship on the page must owe a lot to the real experience of father and son. Or is that being sentimental, and falling into a vein of promotional book talk? I ask because *The Road* does have a pitiless grace in which the sanctity of relationships, and even humanity, begin to seem far-fetched. That wife did kill herself, and the boy is not free from that idea.

But it is beautiful, I think—even if the code of beauty may have been overrated. Beauty is tricky.

"He carried him across the field, stopping to rest each fifty counted steps. When he got to the pines he knelt and laid him in the gritty duff and covered him with the blankets and sat watching him. He looked like something out of a deathcamp. Starved, exhausted, sick with fear. He leaned and kissed him and got up and walked out to the edge of the woods and then he walked the perimeter round to see if they were safe."

In the diagnosis of one short paragraph, may I note the unnecessary but essential "counted" taking us into the man's panting head. Then recognize the rural knowledge in "duff," normally a kind of sweet pudding, but it can be decaying vegetable matter covering ground beneath trees. The ordinary reader may guess at that (we are not thrown), but the inventiveness of the word reminds us, look, this is language. I believe "deathcamp" is startling and a sign that there are camps in this road time beyond what we think we know. Then there is the lilting rhythm in "Starved, exhausted, sick with fear," as if to tell us loveliness can lift the worst topics. "Kissed," I believe breaks your heart, but it is not the same minus "leaned." There is the repetition of "walked," and the inward agreement that being "safe" is only an idea or an ideal, like Vermeer trying to paint Auschwitz.

Old lady: This is teaching me to read.

Author: Or write.

Old lady: And this is all through the book?

Author: Like a river, like the light.

Old lady: I had not seen how beautiful it could be.

Author: You were busy with the story and the threat.

Old lady: I was. I am.

Author: That is natural and proper.

Old lady: Every sentence has this refinement?

Author: And the rhythm. It is why we read it, I think, when the subject is unbearable.

Old lady: The beauty, perhaps, is what keeps the writer at his task.

Author: You do not need to be taught.

Old lady: So the author must dread the completion of his book.

Author: He has his problem, his dead end.

◆

To study writing closely runs the risk of making the writing seem studied. Yet how can any reader or writer live with the thought that this thing happens spontaneously, like a crow chatting to the sky? Doesn't the very word "crow," and the sound of it, signal a kind of ominousness that hardly needs the thrilled premonition in the strings of Bernard Herrmann? How can the end of the world be lovely, or able to balance *Disaster* and *Mon Amour?*

I have chosen to study *San Andreas* and *The Road* in this book as manifestations of my subject because they seem so much at odds. One is a sensationalist movie, a spectacular; the other is not so much written as engraved in our mind, as if our inwardness is the tombstone ready to be placed. But they have things in common, even if you may feel disposed to say that the creator of one is a genius while the gang that made the other are just a bunch of brilliant kids. The standoff between the gangster and the genius is a good way of telling the American story.

Then think how much the two have in common. *San Andreas* was very expensive to make, but it repaid that gamble many times over, only indicating what a wise prophet there is in Steven Mnuchin. *The Road*, too, was a hit. The novel won the Pulitzer Prize and the James Tait Black Memorial Prize. It was a selection of the Oprah Winfrey Book Club. It was the object of enormous critical praise, and it was a big seller, if not quite best—you can't expect everyone to eat duff. And intense, mind-blasting care had gone into both works. That attentiveness in one case involved several hundred people engaged in work so intricate and technical that no one but an expert could follow it, or even see it. Whereas in the other case, even with the example of a young son, there was no doubt that a single person, the author, had dragged this book out of the jungle of his mind and made it as elegant as a cobra.

So the comparison asks us are we more fond of the collective than the master? *San Andreas* is a collaborative work, rich in crowd scenes, and it is delirious and streamlined: in watching it I get some of the elation I feel in watching Fred and Ginger float across a polished floor to the sound of their clacking heels (crows?) and the melody of "I Won't Dance," or Fred and Cyd Charisse in "Dancing in the Dark." It is bliss, dependent on stupidity and the ferment and froth of computer-generated imagery, and I am a sucker for the droll cut from complete mayhem to "Now we rebuild." I love that stupidity. Further, I feel sorely tempted by the surrealism of a dream scene in *The Road* where they trudge out of rain and gloom to find what seems like an abandoned movie theatre. Except that the place is playing *San Andreas* in a flawless print and the two of them sit together in the empty place stunned by the Wow of it.

There is no contest between these two works. We can feel bound to them both, and there is a way in which each serves as useful antidote to the other. But there is another kind of answer to their juxtaposition. *The Road* is founded in a sense of human beings as intense as its reverence for language. When the man kisses the boy, that is not just paternal but an honoring of a code of human resemblance and sympathy that reaches far beyond the swift, trite reunification of the family in *San Andreas*. The film's exuberant willingness about wiping out so many stick figures—to spread disaster like a good jam—comes out of an instinct that all humans are the equivalent of sticks. This is not said reproachfully—the chorus line of victims is as sprightly and willing as any line of Radio City chorines.

But the difference should be noted. McCarthy's measured prose feels the vulnerability of the wife, the man, and the boy with an unhealed wounding. This road place is like Eden after its fall. In other words, Cormac McCarthy is a sentimentalist despite his grim manner, and all praise to him for that. It is a remembered religious echoing that lets the meticulousness of his prose stop short of being a grindstone.

But he is wrong or forlorn, and I think he knows it. The road is a world where books and language have been surpassed and put away. This is enough to make old ladies out of the culture of the Library.

"FUCK OFF, DISASTER!"

Towards the end of June—those can be saddening words if you think of June as the best of summer, the moment when the light does its best to last and there is freshness left in the air.

American numbers were bad in June 2020. Without ERAs and RBIs to mull over, on June 23, there were 2.32 million cases of Covid-19 reported in the country, and 120,000 deaths. At that rate, the 134,000 deaths predicted by August 1 would be surpassed. Can you imagine? For there were surges of infection in states that had not been badly affected at first. Would there be a resurgence in the fall? Did the administration have the will to employ the testing and the tracking, and even the return of a shutdown, that might ease the numbers until a vaccine could be proved and manufactured? And would it be conceivable or decent for the vaccine to be available for everyone on Earth, at no cost? Or would it follow the trend of privilege of every other medicine we have ever made? Can the world afford 7.6 billion vaccines . . . at $10 or $100 a shot . . . come on, you're good at numbers by now.

It will be a question of how poverty can survive. A truly pragmatic leader, a General Kutuzov, let's say, might argue, "Well, a vaccine is a nice thought—but really it's irrelevant." Just the other day, Count Knochensporne told us that he had recommended less testing so the numbers would seem kinder to his egotistical progress. And as he had always known—it was the one thing on which he was correct—the virus was less important than what he called the economy. The virus could go wild—he could be relaxed with a few million deaths (tyrants juggle with zeros)—but without the buoyancy of the economic engine there was no point in trying, or breathing. A congress of dinosaurs might have gathered once to formulate good health policy and better dietary plans, but it did not matter when their big one came down.

Of course, dinosaurs didn't do conferences, but 66 million years later (more or less), self-consciousness had set in. So it was in the month of May, the generality of Americans had not heard of George Floyd, Rayshard Brooks, Ahmaud Arbery, or Breonna Taylor. Correction: Breonna Taylor had been shot and killed by police in Louisville, Kentucky, on March 13, 2020, but not so many had been impressed yet. She had been in her bed with her lover just after midnight, when three plainclothes police forced entry in her house on a no-knock warrant. The boyfriend (who was licensed to have a gun) fired at the intruders, and Taylor was shot eight times. It turned out the cops had come to the wrong house; the person those police were looking for lived somewhere else. The official police report on the incident was a package of lies and omissions. This *was* reported; objections were raised; but it did not spark the air yet or dispute the abject understanding that such things happened to black people.

That waited on the murders of George Floyd and Ahmaud Arbery, and after those the world of America—and its relationship with the mirror—had altered. After how many decades, "we" had discovered that we disapproved of racism, yet the tumor had waited so long. There were demonstrations all over the country, notably in Minneapolis, Louisville, Los Angeles, New York, and Washington, D.C., and the racist faction in society said they were the work of rioters and looters, of extreme radical movements intent on tearing the country apart. Instead ideas gained ground, with hit-record speed, that maybe we didn't need police so much as skilled social workers.

The action of those few weeks seized attention. One could watch Ali Velshi and others from MSNBC on the front lines, affected by tear gas, and subject to demonstrators who had an urge to get on camera, as if being on camera still mattered. It was notable that Fox did not have many reporters on the streets, yet that network elected to portray violent demonstrations and "looters." There were people who broke into stores and carried away stolen goods. But by May 2020 the events on the street overlapped with a country where many were out of work, at risk of losing their place to live. They were also poor and hungry, unprivileged and afraid. This was predictable: in the pandemic, people of color and poverty were more likely to be infected, less able to shelter at home, and with their customary privilege of dying early. The underlying pandemic in the United States—so pervasive it was fanciful to think of treating it—was poverty.

In general, the demonstrations handled themselves very well. They rejected violence, or police provocation. They sensed that the public was catching on to what was a very old cause. They let their momentum develop gradually. So it was the spasms of authority that behaved stupidly.

The worst display of that occurred in Washington, D.C., on the evening of June 2. It was then that the president gave authority for police and national guardsmen to clear Lafayette Square, using tear gas, so that Bone Spurs could take a ponderous, power walk to St. John's Episcopal Church and hold up a Bible. He was leading a small posse that included the chairman of the Joint Chiefs of Staff, General Mark Milley, wearing fatigues; Attorney General William Barr (a sad sack seeming to audition for the role of Vag); the sparkling Kushners; and his own chronic press secretary, Kayleigh McEnany. This was so naïve an attempt at television assertion that it was akin to some of Goya's etchings of disaster, a companion piece to his sonnet on disinfectant.

There was a further travesty to come: the second damnation in the Trump Ring Cycle. In Tulsa, Oklahoma, on June 20, he staged a rally to reelect himself, without noticing the astonishing gathering of ordeals for most Americans. This took place at a 19,000-seat auditorium; the campaign had promised it would be full and overflowing, no matter that Covid was flourishing in Tulsa. The president's 1 hour, 50-minute speech included a 15-minute section—an aria of self-pity and depraved narcissism—in which he played out the embarrassment he had had walking off a ramp at the West Point commencement he had addressed. This had to be a testing point for the news; could these disasters be shown in full for anyone with time to watch, and could the candidacy of the demagogue be valid still after helpless long shots of empty seats? Sixty-two hundred people were present in that Tulsa arena, and some of them looked lost. Within three weeks, there was a trampoline soaring in Covid cases around Tulsa.

Or would America sail on, impoverished, threatened by plague and having to decide whether Black Lives Matter was a cry that could reform the nation, or just a slogan to be stamped on T-shirts or tarmac. Above all, how would this regenerated vocabulary face up to the real event and foreboding—for which the shock of 2020 might be an ungainly rehearsal—the inroads of our weather?

◆

June 2020, so long ago. From where you are now, it may look as remote as the Black Death or as fit for nostalgia as Stan and Ollie laboring up those stairs. By June 24, New York and New Jersey had imposed a 14-day quarantine on travelers from several other states. The European Union was contemplating a similar restriction on would-be visitors from the United States. So more and more of us might be sitting at our table with solitaire and *War and Peace,* or *Death in the Afternoon* and a glass of mineral water.

There was this numbness, and it was hard to decide whether it was restful or fatal. This is an overlooked but deeply felt state, not sure if we are asleep, or being dreamed.

Writers work in different ways, but I am inclined to let a ferment build inside me as ideas circulate like scorpions in a jar. This can be disturbing—to a point of despair, with thoughts of self-termination (and self-dramatizing, of course). But then sometimes if I sit still, I can feel the storm coming to rest, not quite calm but poised. And then I have a habit of turning on the television and sitting with a remote, working my way through channels, like a patient fish going towards a sea.

I have been scolded for this somnolent habit, and I have given up trying to explain that it seems a response to the mechanism of television. Nor do I stress how much I revel in the automatic editing and fragmentary disconnects, until some form begins to emerge, a story that requires me. That's how I rediscovered this classic and its water. See if you know it.

We are looking at a still pond on an October afternoon. It's Sunday, after lunch. The parents are inside the house somewhere between leafing through the papers, dozing, or thinking idly of their indolent potential as lovers. Their two children, a little girl and her older brother, are playing in the large, untidy garden. That's where the pond is.

The little girl wears a bright red plastic raincoat. The boy is on a bicycle. She is floating a ball on the pond.

The girl drowns. The father, inside the house, has some in-tuition or premonition—don't we always imagine the worst as parents? He rushes out into the garden. His son is crying in alarm. The father plunges into the muddy pond. Wetness clings to him. But it is too late. When he hauls up the body of his daughter she is wrapped in weed. He is crying out, though we hardly hear him. His mouth is agape, like a scream in *Battleship Potemkin* or in a Francis Bacon painting. The worst has happened. It is more than the word "disaster" can ever contain. Those who have suffered disaster seldom resort to that melodramatic word.

Yet a hundred yards away, unaware, another happy family may be laughing in the car as they drive to have tea with Grannie somewhere in Hertfordshire. Such cuts are always available.

The parents are called Baxter, John and Laura, Donald Suth-erland and Julie Christie. Of course, it's a movie, so their ideal look can be assumed, but these two were uncommonly lovely in 1973. He had long curly hair for the part. Before she took off any clothes, we knew she was as beautiful as any woman had been on film. They were both well dressed. John has a blue coat that is one of the most desirable garments in cinema. It may seem tact-less to mention this in a story where John is in such agony in the pond reaching for his daughter. But the movie stresses his coat (and colored scarves) repeatedly. It is a coat to die for. As for Laura, she is so slim and her pants are terminally elegant. It is evident that beneath her fashionable brown sweater she has no bra. I am listing these things, but they are meant to be noticed. Whatever their grief, or shock, these two are sexually alert.

And they are a clue that something odd is afoot in *Don't Look Now*—that's the name of the film, and it's an unnerving title for a movie. What makes the clue disconcerting is the feeling that within the obvious disaster this couple are being eroticized. Is their tragedy part of their allure?

After the disaster, the loss, immediately, we find John and Laura in Venice. His work is in the restoration of Renaissance churches and he is in Venice on assignment. Laura has gone with him. She has no job of her own; her role is to be his wife.

It took me years and several viewings of the film, for my troubled thoughts to gather. The Baxters are staying in a smart hotel, and their clothes match the decor. But I came to wonder that bereaved parents would take such care over their appearance. Is it sentimental to suppose that for years they would hardly know what they were wearing, let alone seem such models?

There's something not quite right, but it's hard to know whether it was intended (by director Nicolas Roeg), or is it accidental? Then another worry dawns: they have gone to Italy, leaving their son—a young boy—at an English boarding school. I can't assure you that such a thing could not happen in life: in England and in other cultures there can be class codes that choose not to let emotion show too much. So you get on with life. But a film is so essentially selected that one cannot ignore the implications. Put it this way: in that predicament, I don't think one could endure life with a last child living in another country. Even so, it took me years to work this out and to ask: was there something wrong in the film, or were the Baxters in love with risk?

The film does not tell us how long before Venice the drowning occurred—the pond was filmed at a country house in an autumnal Hertfordshire. But it seems to be no more than a few months earlier. And it's not that decent people can't reassemble their lives in that time, or put on brave faces. But the film cuts from Hertfordshire to Venice so that the abruptness cannot be fobbed off. The recovery is curiously sudden. You can tell yourselves that the two actors are playing it just a touch depressed, but Julie Christie smiles at him like someone in love—or locked in love.

That's far from all, as you likely know or recall. For I am coming to the most famous thing about *Don't Look Now*. Its rapture. One evening in their hotel room, without talk or decisions, John and Laura make love. To put it another way, they embark on what was for 1973 the most explicit or radical sex scene yet done in a mainstream film. It became notorious and harder to look at in its own right, or for the sake of its bereaved people.

The actor and the actress go naked—though in the convention of movies still applicable fifty years later that exposes more of Christie than of Sutherland. They do not really speak, though there are sighs or moans—you cannot have those exhalations without degrees of consent or support. There was discussion at the time as to whether Christie and Sutherland had been "doing it." I see no evidence of that, yet there is a surpassing intimacy and affection between them that is unusual in movie love scenes. So often such things are only sex scenes.

The simulation is credible and arousing, even if we are aware that the framing has been scrupulously managed to avoid glimpses of pubic hair. Why is the system afraid of that growth? Is that why that hair is so often removed in pornography?

It is not exactly a scripted scene. Roeg would say later that it was nearly improvised, out of a feeling that at least one scene of warmth was needed to balance scenes in which the couple argued. But I don't find those disputes in the picture, and I wonder if the whole enterprise had some notion of an unprecedented lovemaking show? Such intercourse is not in the Daphne Du Maurier short story that inspired the film—in that story the daughter has died from illness, not drowning. It is not an attack on cinema to remark on how often it grants itself amour *and* disaster together.

So the players came nervously to the set in dressing gowns. These were discarded and for a crew of three—Roeg, the cinematographer, and a focus-puller (fussy accuracy is erotically essential)—the actors lay down on a bed and more or less did what they thought of, with Roeg calling out orders, like a drill sergeant—"Touch her there—Close your eyes." Et cetera. The collision was shot and choreographed, and the two players were encouraged to be as natural or uninhibited as possible. Have you ever made love for a crew? Would it be love, do you think, in that clash of privacy and performance? Did they do it? What do lovers do except be together and dream of affinity or a thought of dying?

The scene reminds me of the opening to *Hiroshima Mon*

Amour. There is the same timeless sense of bodies in their desirous sleep.

Is this the first time the Baxters have made love since the disaster? Is there some unspoken feeling that they might start another child? Do they need to reassert their passionate relationship? Are they in defiance of catastrophe, as if to shout out at fate, "Fuck off, disaster! You don't frighten me!"

And you probably don't need reminding that the average male ejaculation (Donald Sutherland might be a little above par) shoots about 350 million sperm into a woman. Give or take, and I hope "shoots" is not prejudicial.

There is still another aspect to the scene, a way of cutting. As if in fear of a censor's interference, Roeg added a curious extra. Thus the flow of lovemaking is intercut with precise, close-up shots of the characters getting dressed afterwards to go out. They had slipped out of their clothes like swimmers in water. But the dressing afterwards is formal or businesslike and a resumption of solitude that lovers feel after they have made love. You can call this a trick of editing, a stylish, offsetting device. But the restoration of order conveys an odd sense of the passion having been a moment for hire—a prostitutional arrangement or like the masquerade of two actors. It makes the sex provisional or rather chilly, and it adds to the way we cannot quite reconcile what John and Laura have done here with their loss. But we all have to overcome disaster, or treat it as a trivial plaything.

You see, no matter how spectacular the show, we do not matter.

I believe now that this sequence, the taking clothes off and then putting them back, *is* the film. So I am leaving out a good deal of *Don't Look Now*. It has occultish episodes and then a grisly murder close to horror as a dwarf in a red raincoat turns on John in the night streets of Venice—hideous but tidy? Some esteem the picture for this thrill, but I think it only depletes or distracts us from the nub of the matter: an insinuating portrait of how these two people come to terms with their disaster. But it is in shrugging off the cockamamie plot elements that I have found myself sinking into the more gripping and dangerous idea in the film— that John and Laura did neglect the daughter who drowned. That pond was not safe. They should not have let her play there alone.

But we *are* alone; it is the safety of caring that is an illusion.

Look at the film enough and a slippage occurs—call it a cut or a dissolve—so that we wonder if they were not fucking as the child drowned. Now that is shocking—far more than the horrific ending of the film—but I think it tells us something about the recklessness and the drama in which we may court the most dreadful mishaps.

We insist that they cannot be coincidental.

Of course, Nicolas Roeg did not make this film I am supposing; I doubt he intended or dreamed of it. But intention in cinema is like morning mist before the noon heat of our attention. The parts of the film lay together like bodies. We are not quite as terrified of disaster as we say. We accept that we are bookended by the violence of birth and death. And we are fond of such rituals, especially when they happen to people as pretty as the Baxters.

NECESSITY

Necessity can be a desperate matter, and in what may serve as a kind of handbook for negotiating disaster, I advise you to do what you can in avoiding the blunt challenge (and allure) of having no other option.

But it *is* tricky, and even comic: the pilgrim strolling across a pleasant field, thinking heyday and halcyon, may pause in midstride when he remembers that he has to die. This is nothing personal or punitive; any Thursday will do. But it has always been a necessary part of the bargain over all the delights in being born. As the pilgrim says to himself, if I have a mother and a father—and if in the advances of science those figures still seem necessary—aren't they going to have to die?

One might wish to avoid that necessity. Thinking of it on one's walk may bring down strain or fatigue. Or the occasional loss of hope. There's humor in that predicament, but anger too.

That's one reason why we try to maintain some amour in the night.

Part of the trickiness in this matter is that we have worked out a cult of necessity, a way of worshiping it and employing it as a model for what we do—or what we have to do. Night and day we are looking for mechanisms that let us escape responsibility or choosing. We rejoice in Stan and Ollie following the order of getting that piano up the steps. We believe in exhausted geniuses discovering a precious vaccine. People say that poor old Vincent Van Gogh just *had* to paint, no matter the damage, the grief, and the insanity he spread around him like a shadow from his sun. In a similar way, that chronically inventive man Orson Welles was compelled on a self-destructive career that could only show us how he was at odds with himself. We may be bewildered by Vincent at $75 million a frame, or by *Citizen Kane* cornering the grand prix of cinema. Our civilization doesn't really wish that Vincent had been a diligent but ordinary postman (like Joseph Roulin), or that Orson had spent fifty years composing chess puzzles for the local paper in Kenosha, Wisconsin.

No, they were driven by necessity, and we revel in what that pressure produced. But that is tricky: it may be that under the same imperative some other Wisconsinite wrote ponderous, unpublishable novels all his life, so that his neglected children withered and perished in blind intensity. It may even be that another painter, an Austrian, in his 1920s stroll across a sweet meadow, realized that he might need to kill us all. More or less.

And a lot of parents might prefer their children to be quiet, humdrum nonentities, happy now and then, or uncomplaining, instead of the demons who seem on fire because of what they have to do, crouched and furious under the burden of necessity.

I am reminded of the novel *Rogue Male*, by Geoffrey Household, published in 1939, in which a skilled English sportsman finds himself in a dense European forest, with his rifle, close enough to see the Monster in his sights. Will he fire? Should he do so? Even in 1939, a good deal of disaster was known and understood. A great deal more might have been imagined. This sportsman is stopped before he can decide (thus necessity is finessed) by the Monster's thugs. There are movies of this story, like Fritz Lang's *Man Hunt* (1941), where Walter Pidgeon is the sportsman. Far better is the 1976 picture *Rogue Male*, in which Peter O'Toole is radiant as the man with the rifle.

Those looming figures never quite depart our stage. So it was in the years from 2015 on that I began to realize how a vain, tasteless, dishonest disaster might be more than he deserved; if some power and force of necessity dropped on his golden head, it might be enough to inspire him. Thus in the next few years the Monster acquired an ecstatic dishonesty, a vibrant cruelty, an indifference to his job and its tasks, a lyric sense of himself as dangerous, pandemonium with its finger on a trigger. Not just a very bad man. He had this extra menace—it is immense, a San Andreas fault—that he and our system had given him a charm so that millions of us would vote for him and hold him in some amour.

There was a climate then that longed to bypass necessity—for very persuasive reasons. It said, don't worry or get upset, the Monster is just an aberration, a foolishness, a specter that will burn off in the noon sun. It's only four years, this mood said in an encouraging way, as if unmindful that 1941, 1942, 1943, and 1944 were just four years. So while I played along with the pleasantness of life, I did start to conjure up a scenario in which I might be the sportsman. If, by wretched mischance, I happened to find myself in the same forest as the Monster, I could feel drawn to dispose of him. There might be a weight of obligation in that feeling. This would not be out of dislike of him but from a desire to save so many others from him.

I realized this was not just an unwholesome way of wondering; it was against my nature. I would be too much of a coward or dreamer to let myself fall into such a situation—the space, the room where he was waiting, hovering, wondering if it was his day for assassination and ready to take vengeance for it. Rather than be in the same building with the Monster, I would take a trip to Nova Zembla. So the idea of any actual intervention was a foolish joke, if you like, a whimsy.

But the sharp air of necessity did not recede. Indeed, it began to be apparent that there were ways in which this Monster meant to kill us. While leering at our faint resolve with his cynic's gaze, he was dreaming not just of murder, but of massacre. He regarded us as mere audience; he could not conceive of the community of a nation he measured only on a scale of his mythic greatness. Wasn't he presiding over a plague with fatuous indifference? Hadn't he led an assault on our government and its servants? How many children had been severed from their families? How many had died from Covid in his neglect? Wasn't it emerging that the passion in a narcissist was ready for anyone else to die? Or everyone?

Of course, that was long ago. That darkness passed, just as those with crossed fingers promised it would. But you never know. Necessity plots its game every time a Delaware falls off the polar ice block. The father in *The Road* might come upon a man threatening his son and be unable to resist the necessity of using his last bullet to shoot down that man, no matter that he proved to be a Mr. Rogers. There's always a dark joke to get us off the stage.

But pray that necessity doesn't find you and insist on respect.

THE TABLE

Old lady: That makes me grim.

Author: That can be a measure of affection.

Old lady: I remember that, but—

Author: I beg you—look!

Old lady: Great heavens, sir, I never saw a table so long. What do you propose to do with it?

It is a rare table made of infinite DISSOLVING.

I had it constructed by a learned and ingenious craftsman named Alexander Selkirk. It was while being disastrously marooned four years and four months on a south Pacific island that he developed his skills as a carpenter, and now he is in business up in northern California, in the Whiskeytown area, where the great trees grow. So I went to him with my venture and he gazed at me in that calm spirit of a Scotsman (he had been born in Fife, between the firths of Tay and Forth), or of anyone who has been so alone for four years.

He was calculating the pines that might be required and he asked me, "What length do you foresee for this table of yours?"

I told him I was thinking of a hundred yards.

He gave no sign of dismay or incredulity. He did not waver, as if he was himself a pine. He did not so much as smile. I could see from his eyes that he was already set on calculations, not just over the properties of pine, but on the degrees of insanity. How many trees? What length of span? How far apart would the supports need to be? These were intricate prospects to ponder.

My order would have defeated lesser men. But I knew my Selkirk, and I recalled that in his isolation he had tamed feral goats, fed on wild turnips, and made comfortable huts out of the timber and the duff on his island.

You may wonder why he was there. He had been a sailor on the *Cinque Ports*. And being both a shrewd judge of ships but someone who never learned to restrain intemperate opinions, he told the inexperienced captain of the vessel that it was unsound and would founder. Disaster was only a step or two away. Well, the raw captain of the *Cinque Ports* had been irked by these prophecies, and when they did not cease he decided to save Selkirk from any mishap by casting him away on the next damn desert island they found.

This duly happened. Selkirk was granted a musket with powder and shot and a few basic tools—a knife, a cooking pot, needle and thread—and a Bible. And he was left there.

I should tell you that shortly thereafter the *Cinque Ports* did sink.

Enough of that. I simply wanted to explain that my choice of Selkirk was no whim or caprice. He was the man for the job. And the table now is proof of that. What a marvel it is! Yes, it is a hundred yards long, built of exceptional lengths of pine that have been planed to a smoothness like that of skin. The table is four feet wide, no more, and a hundred yards long, with simple trestle supports every twelve feet. It has to be seen to be believed. Even then, you may wonder.

"Well," said Selkirk on the day I went up to his place to take receipt of the work—it was a fine day, though not remarkable— "it'll be some kind of a feast you'll be having at your table. Do you know enough folk to fill it?"

I tried to explain that I was in no way averse to the prospect of a feast (though I was uncertain where we'd get the chairs), and as to the size of my circle, why not invite every reader? However, a banquet was not my prime intention. The table was to serve another purpose.

"What can that be?" asked Selkirk, still without a smile, though I thought I saw a wriggle at the right-hand corner of his mouth.

You see, my readers, I had devised the table for you. I am in need of an ample model, pushing the bounds of belief and possibility, but still manageable in terms of vision and accomplishment. After all, a man, a Bolt, can run the length of my immense table in about nine and a half seconds and a woman needs only a second more—that's what Florence Griffith-Joyner managed in 1988—10.49 seconds.

Enough of that: digressions clamor for attention.

My table had this intent, and I explained it to Selkirk in the way I am telling you. The history of this Earth goes back 4.5 billion years. Give or take—no one can be certain of whatever 10:49 a.m. it was that our matter gathered out of whatever materiality had existed before. I have not the least ability or intention of explaining why 4.5 billion years—that does not interest me. I am unimpressed, if you know what I mean, so long as you understand the dumb awe I feel for the fact.

"Ah," said Selkirk, "and how long I wonder was it before we started playing golf?" Not a glimmer of a smile. These are the comedians worth having. There is an intriguing book to be done, a history of comics who were devout about not smiling or laughing. One day, perhaps.

Well, I told Selkirk—we were sharing shot glasses of single malt to mark the delivery of the table—as a matter of testified fact, the very first appearance on our Earth of what you might call our ancestors, rather solemn apelike fellows who walked and wondered, was only six million years ago.

"They were looking for a lost ball, no doubt," said Selkirk.

But people like Cary Grant, human beings, more or less, began to appear as lately as 200,000 years ago. "As for golf," I added, I had looked this up, "there is a legend of it from just before 1300."

Selkirk seemed perplexed. "I thought I had invented it on my island," he said. He apologized. He had another client to see. He had been engaged to make a raft, big enough for three good golf holes, a par three, a four, and a five, with a clubhouse, a platform on which gentlemen might take to the water in the event of some cataclysm.

Farewell Alexander. Let me tell you about the table (his greatest work, so far).

To be blunt about it, I want this table to stand for the history of the Earth: that would be 4.5 billion years—now you fear the conversationalist is giving way to the didact—represented in 100 yards. I'll save you the time and the mathematical struggle: with my table, 1 yard of pine, as blond as Charlize Theron, must stand for 45 million years. Take that a step farther—a single inch of our pine is the equivalent of 1.25 million years. So you can imagine how much table will serve for the six million years I spoke about: it would be, give or take, the length of a modestly erect penis.

As for the 200,000 years (the slow dawn of conversation, Shakespeare, single malts, and golf), that would need about a sixth of an inch, or the space between this word and that one.

◆

The lesson of the table may be humiliating. How can our self-importance be so minute? If you want to regard us as the stars of the show, instead of uncounted trees. And for the moment at least we seem to find that human beings do ride on a seesaw that goes from glory to disaster, from happiness to its black hole. So it is generally a characteristic—or even an essential—in disaster studies that someone must survive the extinction event to sing the song, "I was moved . . . and I will start again." We are not ourselves without that sense of franchise and a pivotal position in history.

So it is that as the *Pequod* is dragged down into the vortex (that is what Melville says), Ishmael finds himself in the ocean ready to join all the drowned crewmates:

"Round and round, then, and ever contracting towards the button-like black bubble at the axis of that slowly wheeling circle, like another Ixion I did revolve. Till, gaining that vital centre, the black bubble upward burst; and now, liberated by reason of its cunning spring, and, owing to its great buoyancy, rising with great force, the coffin life-buoy shot lengthwise from the sea, fell over, and floated by my side. Buoyed up by that coffin, for almost one whole day and night, I floated on a soft and dirge-like main. The unharming sharks, they glided by as if with padlocks on their mouths; the savage sea-hawks sailed with sheathed beaks. On the second day, a sail drew near . . ."

That ship was the *Rachel*, which makes me smile, because I have a daughter of that name. Chance is always swimming in our water. So surely it is a trick of irony and primed coincidence that Ishmael survives by clinging to a coffin. Melville's book is a place where metaphor taunts the liberty that people like to think is theirs. And so Ishmael survives to tell the whole story, just as Alexander Selkirk inspired Defoe to write *Robinson Crusoe*. I feel no resentment at Melville's trickery. It's hard to write a book without that kind of coincidence, or the looming theorem of the table.

So you might look at my table and its smooth surface and note that there is this curious whorl in the wood—could it be a face?—and there it is again, a billion and a half years earlier. So you could act upon the resemblance and call it significance. But if we do our best simply to countenance the length of the table and the barely visible flourish of human performance, isn't it easier or more natural to conclude that we hardly matter?

But no, you must protest, we cannot be so callous or so casual. Even Ahab, that Satanic figure, must have fumed at how the whale had defeated him, still, he had an instant to know he had been hanged on his own harpoon rope. The horror—and the irony; it's a pretty demise for a skipper. Those children in their school at Aberfan as their day began may have seen or heard the avalanche coming up to their window, and then the panic and a scattered childish prayer . . .

We cannot give up on the imaginative effort, the sympathy, that wonders what it's like to be disastered. In 2020, millions of us considered the peculiar plight of Covid-19, the way in which you might be taken into hospital, treated by health workers who are increasingly concealed by their protective clothes, and you are unable to be touched by your dear ones because they cannot risk infection. That loneliness might hasten death, it is so terrible to contemplate. And so some smart people had the idea of putting photographs of the doctors and nurses on their protective clothes simply so the patients had a face and a person to fix on.

Disaster cries out for witness. Somehow Melville felt he could not simply tell the story. He needed the patient Ishmael at the beginning and the end to say, Look, this is what happened. I am alive!

But it's hard in the context of the table to feel for the terror of all the people who have died in disaster—which may be close to saying all the people who have died. It is part of our ignominy that we do not remember and may be incapable of registering all the sorrow. So we told ourselves, be calm, my dear, the Lord sees it all. We are so desperate for calm.

Because of my age and time, Aberfan was a crucial disaster, and it is a woeful tale. But some of you will not have known about the event—after all, that Wales was long ago and far away, and its death toll is modest compared with the losses in the Indian Ocean tsunami. There is ample literature on the experience of the Holocaust and I will not get over my cultural infection from it. I mean the dismay that felt its ash was on the ground forever. But it is conceit or contrivance to say I feel the same for the dead in the Black Death, for the morgue called Slavery, or from disasters that I have never heard of. And on the table, the space between the Holocaust and the Black Death—six hundred years or so—is a scratch on the surface, too slight to see.

We want lives to matter (especially those that have not had the weight of fame—in other words, most of us, most of them). As of now, sentiment may be our most precious or idealized trait—but we fear how that treasury can turn sentimental. I know Joan of Arc was burned alive at the stake in Rouen in 1431. It is possible—from medical literature—to research what occurs to the body

and the organism in being burned alive. I'm thinking of how long
it takes, the frenzy and the pain, the great difficulty even a saint
would have in crediting God's calm survey as her flesh bubbled
and her hair ignited. Joan didn't know she was a saint yet.

In 1957, it was said that the actress Jean Seberg was "scorched"
while shooting Joan's burning for the film *Saint Joan*. She appeared in danger for a few seconds. Or was that just public relations alarm to promote a movie? The picture was a flop and
Seberg seemed adrift. Then she rallied and became significant,
getting **bold** type in the columns, so that an autopsist would pay
attention when, in September 1979 (she was only forty), her body
decomposed in a Renault parked in the 16th arrondissement in
Paris. That decay had taken eight or nine days before the police
ripped the car open and its stench invaded the street.

The distress of others is another country. We partake in it as
avid onlookers and greedy spies. The acuity of disaster in tragic
narratives, and in the News genre, is that it has happened to
other people. I alone survived—the Ishmael dividend. It's a fearsome interruption that befalls Marion Crane at the Bates motel,
but we watch it every time. It is meaningful in terms of our own
distress. The advance of humanity cannot really matter, but we
make lifelong efforts to inflate our loss and our pain. We long
to signify. So our existence slips towards pathos or the elated fun
over a cock-and-bull story. The table is long enough for despair
and hilarity.

We only know about recent disasters; so we think it's a modern craze. That's a consequence of failing memory. But it has to do with the insecure age of humanism in which we hope to track through our darkness ahead just as we glimpse two thousand or so years into the past. Nothing is more fey in that modernism than the fad for religion (so brief, so gaudy, so cruel, so feeble), in which tongues, texts, and voices tried to insist that the individual human being matters enough to have some god watching us. But in any impersonation of a deity how can we convey the stunning boredom that he or she would have to put up with counting our disasters?

I have tried to keep score, with files of reports on disasters. But I feel guilty because I have omitted so many of them—as if every calamity wouldn't move you to tears if you heard the detail. I remember the final chapter in Hemingway's *Death in the Afternoon*. That 1932 treatise on bullfighting is packed with technical detail and a lucid account of the theatre of the bulls. It seems expert and practical, yet it could be a dream. The book even creates an old lady sitting beside Papa in the stands, commenting on the bullfight and literary matters. But in that last chapter, the author draws back and says, "If I could have made this enough of a book it would have had everything in it." That hope.

And thus he proceeds to make a glorious list of things seen and matters that occurred in his tour of bullfighting. It falls short of "everything," but the gesture is generous and open, and that chapter may be one of the best things he ever wrote. It includes this fragment about his first wife—"Hadley, with the bull's ear wrapped in a handkerchief, the ear was very stiff and dry and the hair all wore off it and the man who cut the ear is bald now too and slicks long strips of hair over the top of his head and he was beau then. He was, all right."

Sentiment poised over sentimentality, like a photograph of a matador, his sword hovering over the bull's shoulders—when such grace and courage must turn into a fatal coup.

I could catalogue so many other disasters, but you've had enough. Already, as we wonder if we can survive the coronavirus, and foresee some climactic confrontation of those who have with those who have not, we understand that 2020 and '21 are a dawning in the complete test of climate intensification and its potential for desolation. We have to have a respect for long views and hope that's not just sentimental.

Think of yourself as Pierre in *War and Peace*. He is caught up in the terrible retreat from Moscow in 1812. Men and plans are dying everywhere. He is walking away from "home"; he feels he is watching the close of a world worth having. But he is holding on, as if attention could yet save us all:

"Everything that Pierre now saw made almost no impression on him—as if his soul, preparing for a difficult struggle, refused to receive impressions that might weaken it."

Will the morning sky be bruised or bloodshot? Do we believe in reading such sights now that weather has turned into screwball schematics? But since it's not yet light or an indicated narrative tendency, then couples can combine again, coalesce, hardly sure if they are awake or being dreamed. Those lovers from Hiroshima, the actors—Eiji Okada and Emmanuelle Riva—are dead now, returned to the ground or to carbon. But their hushed conversation is still urgent and alive.

Perhaps the piano will be delivered today.

ACKNOWLEDGMENTS

Over the last weekend of January 2021, a section of the most beautiful road I have ever driven, Route 1, just south of Big Sur, in California, collapsed into the sea below. There were helicopter gulls getting coverage to let us marvel at the disruption and wonder whether it would be worth rebuilding the road and making it "safe." It had collapsed a few times before and reason begins to question its viability, even if it is a wondrous experience. I remember my friend Mary Corliss, in the passenger seat going south—on the very edge of the world—being exhilarated but desperate at the road. Danger is a thing we remember forever.

In this same January weekend, there were reports from a professor of geophysics at MIT that by 2100 the Earth faced extinction in its carbon cycle; in Washington D.C., there were Republicans in knots trying to persuade themselves that January 6 had been just one of those things; and somehow or other, it was emerging that Americans of color or poverty were having a tougher time finding a vaccine than . . . well, than my wife and I, who had appointments for February 3. It was said a genocidal war was raging in Ethiopia.

Beyond that, we enjoyed an old-fashioned movie, *The Dig*, set in Suffolk in 1939, about the discovery of a buried ship from the sixth century. One marvel of this film was to see how steadily Ralph Fiennes—with gaze, accent, and buttered humility—was himself like an archaeological probe into rural Britain before the Second World War. No, *The Dig* is not a disaster movie, or not obviously so; it's not that challenging. But it's an ode to history that sets you thinking about strangers who died in the sixth century. So it's telling that Carey Mulligan is exquisite as a pale, fragile woman who is not just dying—she's being erased, while leaving her touching smile in the air. This is the eve of war. So many movies use the end of the film to pay homage to the end of the world.

What I am trying to say is that we have digested disaster; it is our music and our rhythm, despite the damage done in its name. So a perverse gratitude is in order to ruin and burial, to those who built Highway 1 and rebuilt it, and to all the gloomy onlookers. You see, I had a good time doing this rueful book, and a lot of people helped.

In the obvious and necessary sense, I am grateful to John Donatich, who supported and edited the book at Yale, who pondered over sentences and matters of fact and tact, and became a friend in the process. Very gently, he pushed and cajoled the book into shapes I hadn't seen. Also at Yale, I was helped by Abbie Storch and Margaret Otzel and reunited with Dan Heaton, who passes under the label copy editor. Anyone who works with him knows that is inadequate. In what he calls his retirement he wonders whether he has become crankier. It doesn't matter. He was always that way. Copy editors need to be pitiless.

But I have never met Dan, not once on four books. That seems odd, but more plausible after 2020, in which I did not see three children and three grandchildren. So many of us have the same stories, and a Zoom gallery to go with them. There are other email and texting relationships full of humor (black is allowed) in which disaster has waited patiently at the foot of the stairs or on the street outside, keeping its private eye on us. That group of friends who helped me through this book—with everything from anecdotes to passing remarks—includes Tom Luddy, Phil Kaufman, Kelly Sultan, Greil and Jenny Marcus, Eleanor Bertino, Elizabeth and Chuck Farnsworth, Diane Johnson, Steve Wasserman, Michael Ondaatje and Linda Spalding, Molly Haskell, Mark Feeney, Douglas McGrath, Michael Barker, Jonathan David Kirshner, Lili Anolik, Bill Holodnak, Leon Wieseltier, Mary Pickering and Hank Lauricella, Max Endersby, Tom Thurman, Mark Kidel. And still Mary Corliss, who scooped my stricken body off her floor in New York in February 2020 before we knew what danger was.

Then there is extended family: Kate and Steve Haines in

Geneva; Mathew (to whom the book is dedicated), Michelle O'Callaghan, Grace, and Joe in Oxford; Rachel and Sean Arnold and Anne in Lewes, with Isaac in Bristol.

There are Nicholas and Annie Bishai in Brooklyn.

Zachary has been living with us during Covid and in the mishap I have come to know him not just as a son but as the best company, a skilled cook, a lovely laugher, and a very close friend.

And Lucy, constant and calm in the room next door.

INDEX

In a sleep clinic, one's unsettled night can be recorded exactly and electronically. So, an index is like that: a gathering of particle facts with the undercurrent of whatever we call dreaming.

Index

education during Covid, 151–52
Edwards, Ethan, 135
Eichmann, Adolf, 122
Eisenstein, Sergei, 5–12
Elizabeth II, 17, 84–89
end of the world, filed under, 41–66
Epstein, Jeffrey, 87
European Union, 173
extinction event, 157

Fabrizio, Andre, 26
Facebook, 49
face masks, 16–17
Fairbanks, Douglas, 25
Fairvale, 6
Faizi, Tatima, 57
Falling Soldier, The, 60–62
Farallon islands, 98
father and son, 70–78, 125–26,
  155–67, 176, 185
Fauci, Dr. Anthony, 26, 136, 138
Fife, 187–88
fires, 16, 45–46, 52–53, 159
firing guns, 7
Fisk, Carlton, 94
Floyd, George, 170–71
Fonda, Henry, 38
Ford, Harrison, 145
Foreign Affair, A, 22
Four Corners, 114–15
Fox News, 97
Foy, Claire, 86
Frank, Anne, 63
French, Daniel Chester, 135
Friedman, Thomas, 49, 109

Gable, Clark, 20
Gaines, Ray, 24–30
gambling, 20, 52
Garbo, Greta, 65

Gardner, Ava, 23
Gates, Bill, 145
Gatorade, 29
Germany Year Zero, 22
Giamatti, Paul, 26
Gilbert, Billy, 7
global warming, 53
Gnazzo, Cory, 101
Godard, Jean-Luc, 48
Golden Gate Bridge, 16, 29, 33,
  108
golf, 68–69, 190–91
Goya, Francisco, 44–45, 62
Grant, Cary, 190
Grapes of Wrath, The, 38
Gray, Lucy, 19, 41, 97–98, 107
Great War, 68
Griffin, Phil, 101
Griffith-Joyner, Florence, 190
Grizzly Man, 46
Guardian, 93
Guernica, 22
Gugino, Carla, 25

Hackl, Karlheinz, 65
Halloween, 43, 48
Hannity, Sean, 98
Harris, Thomas, 123
Harry, Prince, 88
hats, 7, 9
Haverhill, MA, 38, 57
Hayes, Chris, 97
Hayes, Alfred, 50
Hay-on-Wye, 71
Hayward, CA, 24
Heaven's Gate, 18
Hedren, Tippi, 47
Held, Tom, 21
Hemingway, Ernest, vi, 12, 31,
  123–25, 127–29, 196–97. See also